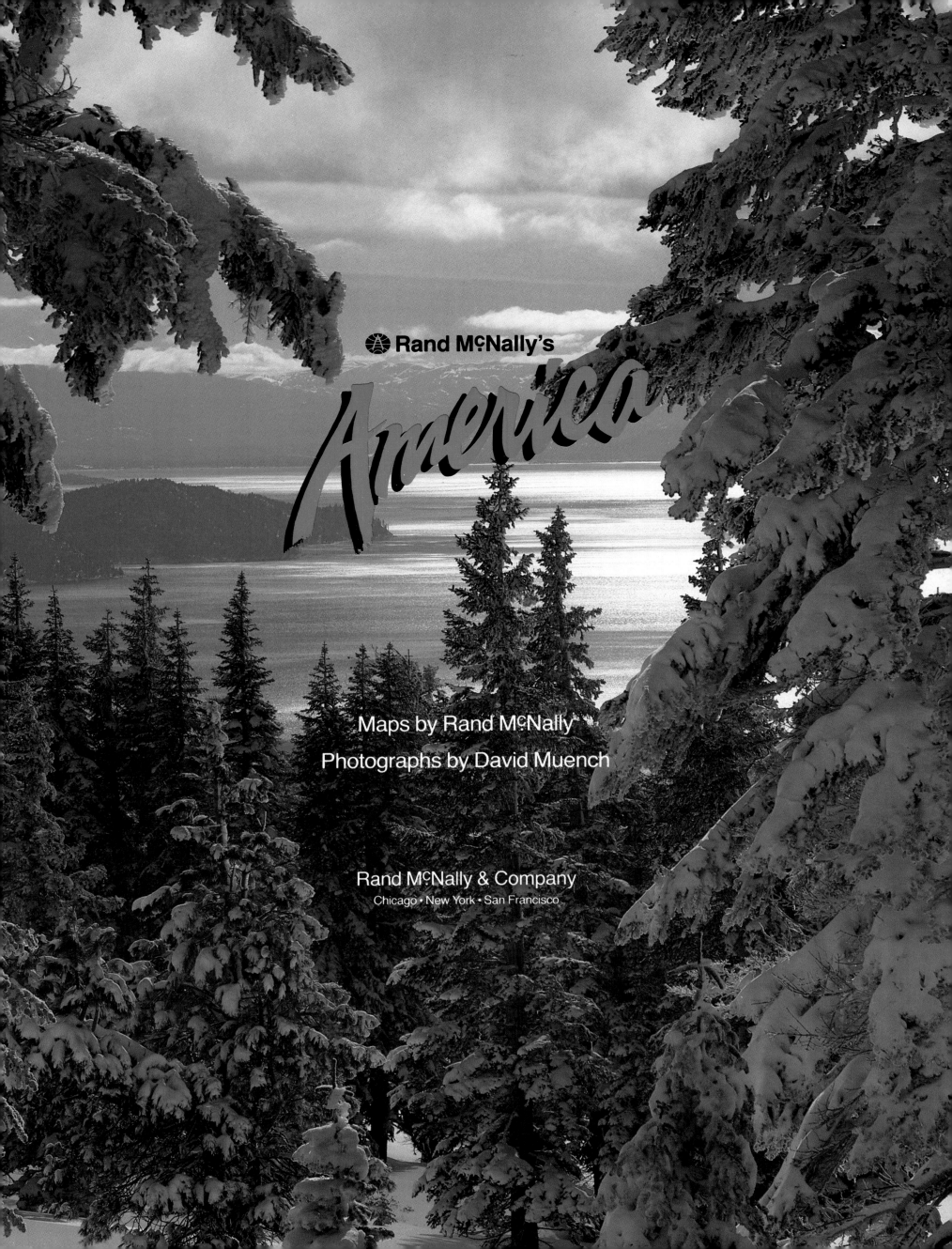

Rand McNally's
America

Maps by Rand McNally

Photographs by David Muench

Rand McNally & Company
Chicago • New York • San Francisco

Overleaf– WINTER AT LAKE TAHOE / CALIFORNIA – NEVADA

Rand McNally's
America

Photographs by David Muench:

Jacket, title page, copyright/contents spread, 8-27, 43, 52-70, 85,93, 95-113, 114 bottom, 119, 121, 129, 140-174, 181, 193, 196-207, 210, 211.

Authors and consultants for the special maps and text:
Dr. Norton S. Ginsberg, Director, East-West Environment and Policy Institute, Hawaii.
Dr. Kenneth E. Foote, Department of Geography, University of Texas at Austin.
Dr. Richard E. Dahlberg, Department of Geography, Northern Illinois University.

Map credits:
41 *Population* Dr. Klaus J. Bayr, Keene State College, New Hampshire. 87 *Small-Town Growth* Dr. Charles T. Zier, Dept. of Geography and Planning, East Carolina University, North Carolina. 139 *Ethnic Diversity* Bulletin of the University of Wisconsin, October 1942.

Map section photo credits:
28 *top* James Blank/FPG; *bottom* Anthony Morganti/FPG.
31 Tom Algire/FPG. 33 DuPont Co. 35 J. Randklev/FPG.
37 Chuck Feil/FPG. 39 *top* J. Blank/FPG; *bottom* Marcus Brooke/FPG.
41 N. Groffman/FPG. 45 Grant Heilman Photography. 47 Grant Heilman Photography. 49 *top* Alastair Black/FPG; *bottom* A. Griffin/ H. Armstrong Roberts. 51 G. Hampfler/H. Armstrong Roberts. 71 W. Metzen/H. Armstrong Roberts. 73 Chevron U.S.A., Inc. 75 Grant Heilman Photography. 77 NASA. 79 A. McGee/FPG. 81 Southern Living/Geoff Gilbert. 83 E. Cooper/FPG. 87 William Felger/ Grant Heilman Photography. 89 Dick Dietrich/FPG. 91 Tennessee Tourist Development. 114 *top* Grant Heilman Photography. 117 Illinois Dept. of Transportation. 123 Grant Heilman Photography. 125 H. Armstrong Roberts. 127 Grant Heilman Photography. 131 Grant Heilman Photography. 133 North Dakota Tourism Promotion Division. 135 Bernard G. Silberstein/FPG. 137 Courtesy of South Dakota Division of Tourism. 135 Edgar G. Mueller. 175 Kent Dannen. 177 Richard C. Towlen/FPG. 179 James Blank/FPG. 183 L. Burton/ H. Armstrong Roberts. 185 J. Messerschmidt. 187 Ray Nelson. 189 W. Metzen/H. Armstrong Roberts. 191 Grant Heilman Photography. 195 Ron Thomas/FPG. 212 Ray Atkeson. 213 Chuck O'Rear/West Light. 215 Ed Cooper/H. Armstrong Roberts. 217 Chuck O'Rear. 219 E. Nagele/FPG. 221 Jim Hosmer. 223 G. Schwartz. Alaska photo pages 208-209 by Jeff Schultz.

Source of population and income statistics:
Market Statistics, S & MM 1988 "Survey of Buying Power."

Rand McNally's America
copyright ©1989 by Rand McNally & Company.
From *This Great Land* and *Atlas of the United States*, copyright ©1983 by Rand McNally & Company.
Second edition, revised.
Second printing, 1990.

Library of Congress Catalog Number: 89-42902
ISBN 0-528-83364-2

SIERRA BLANCA, WHITE SANDS NATIONAL MONUMENT / NEW MEXICO

PORTLAND HEAD LIGHTHOUSE / MAINE

The Northeast

The Northeast

A Stubborn, Enduring Corner of America

STORMY SEAS POUND THE WORN BOULDERS off the coast of Maine, tossing spray high into the air, where it is caught by the fitful sea wind and blown across the tops of the spruce and pine. Across the rolling meadows of Vermont and New Hampshire, ancient fences of fieldstone create strange geometric patterns, and in the low areas there are great thickets of alder, birch, and goldenrod. Curtains of snow move down the rocky shore of the North Atlantic, shrouding the coastlines of Massachusetts, Rhode Island, and Connecticut and bringing a premature darkness to a winter day.

The Northeast possesses the priceless gift of variety. The landscape offers the sea and rivers, great sand dunes, forests and lowlands. Four distinct seasons offer nearly every kind of weather a temperate land can provide. The landscape of New England is rich, with its rivers, lakes, forests, mountains, and seashore. Character moderates and softens as one moves south. New York and Pennsylvania can have cold winters, but autumn lasts longer and spring comes earlier, and the cruel sting of the New England winter is lacking. If there is truly an

alliance between character and climate, the Northeast states would seem to prove it. The clean church spires and village greens of New England persist through New York, northern New Jersey, and Pennsylvania, but are seldom seen further south. And the stringent austerity of the early Calvinists and the Shakers, still an influence in New England, is mellowed by the German Catholics. The Amish of Pennsylvania struggle to retain the purity of the simple life.

Tides control the coastal life of Maine, as the heartbeat maintains life in the body. From Kittery, in southern Maine, to Calais, where the state first touches New Brunswick, Canada, the coastline is less than 250 miles for an airborne creature, but the coves, reaches, bays, and inlets provide the state with 3,478 miles of waterfront—one-half of the tidal line of the entire eastern littoral of the United States.

Inland, the Maine countryside changes abruptly. Gone are the coastal plains; first the country is rolling and then it becomes rough, even primitive. The landscape is dominated by wilderness and lakes, with deep forests and bogs. Wildlife abounds. The north woods is one of the few places in the

Connecticut
Delaware
Maine
Maryland
Massachusetts
New Hampshire
New Jersey
New York
Pennsylvania
Rhode Island
Vermont

nation where landlocked salmon can still be found.

The first escarpments of the massive Appalachian Mountain range rise in western Maine, New Hampshire, Vermont, and New York. The Appalachians are to the East what the Rockies are to the West. Among the oldest mountains on earth, they constitute a nearly continuous chain stretching all the way to Alabama, running roughly parallel to the Atlantic Seaboard.

While the seaboard region, extending from Portland, Maine, to Washington, D.C., has grown to be the third greatest population center in the world, Vermont and most of New Hampshire are largely divorced from the dense urban concentration found closer to the Atlantic Coast. Here the land sweeps westward toward Lake Ontario in a series of neat meadows, rolling hills, and the taller peaks of Vermont's Green Mountain range.

In the deep valley between the Green Mountains and the Adirondacks, where the land drops off to form Lake Champlain and Lake George, is some of America's most majestic country. South of Lake George, the Hudson River valley com-

mences, threaded by the Hudson River, which flows from Lake Tear of the Clouds in the Adirondacks all the way to the Atlantic Ocean at New York Bay. The Hudson's channel is said to extend more than one hundred miles into the ocean to the end of the continental shelf.

New York's fertile river valleys form a gigantic geographical Y, the Hudson being the right arm and the Mohawk River the left. In the Hudson Valley lie some of America's oldest vineyards, which still produce many New York State wines. The state's most famous vineyards are in the Finger Lakes region, on the slopes between Lake Canandaigua and Lake Keuka, where the country — now clear of the mountains — sweeps spaciously toward that thirty-six-mile-wide isthmus that is divided by the Niagara River. Here a freakish drop in the river of 326 feet, most of it in a single, roaring plunge, creates Niagara Falls, still considered one of the wonders of the world.

This is the northeastern corner of America, a stubborn, enduring land, where the continent rises out of the stormy North Atlantic and spreads south and west in majestic mountain ranges, green valleys, and plains.

Overleaf– CAPE COD NATIONAL SEASHORE / MASSACHUSETTS

LAKES OF THE CLOUDS AND RIDGES FROM TOP OF MOUNT WASHINGTON / NEW HAMPSHIRE

STONINGTON HARBOR / MAINE

Top– FIRST SNOW, MOUNT GREYLOCK / MASSACHUSETTS

Bottom– VIEW OF LITTLE RIVER VALLEY, FROM MOUNT MANSFIELD / VERMONT

Left– NIAGARA FALLS / NEW YORK

Above– BUTTERMILK FALLS STATE PARK / NEW YORK

Above– HEART LAKE, ADIRONDACK MOUNTAINS / NEW YORK

Right– BALD CYPRESS, TRUSSUM POND / DELAWARE

ALLEGHENY RIVER FROM TIDIOUTE OVERLOOK / PENNSYLVANIA

Left– BASS HARBOR HEAD, ACADIA NATIONAL PARK / MAINE

Above– BRENTON POINT, NEAR NEWPORT / RHODE ISLAND

Maryland

POPULATION 4,562,600.
Rank: 18.*Density:* 464 people/mi² (179 people/km²).*Urban:* 80.3%.*Rural:* 19.7%.
INCOME/CAPITA $14,693.
Rank: 6.
ENTERED UNION April 28, 1788, 7th state.

CAPITAL Annapolis, 34,600.
LARGEST CITY Baltimore, 757,900.
LAND AREA 9,838 mi² (25,480 km²).
Rank: 42.*Water area:* 623 mi² (1,614 km²).
DIMENSIONS N–S 120 miles, E–W 200 miles.

ELEVATIONS *Highest:* Backbone Mountain, 3,360 ft (1,024 m).*Lowest:* Atlantic Ocean shoreline, sea level.
CLIMATE Hot summers, cool winters; warm summers, cold winters in west. Ample rainfall.

Maryland contains a great deal of economic and cultural diversity within its narrow borders. Its small size and its position on Chesapeake Bay would seem to indicate a relatively unified, even uniform, state. But Maryland is actually a composite of many areas, each reflecting a different tradition of American life.

East of Chesapeake Bay is the low-lying Delmarva Peninsula, shared by and taking its name from Delaware, Maryland, and Virginia. The section of the peninsula lying within Maryland is known as the Eastern Shore, and this area is a strong agricultural and fishing region, supplying products to large population centers to the north and west. But its culture still retains a prominent colonial flavor, reflected in its architecture and social customs. The beauty and seclusion of the peninsula make it attractive to both tourists and new residents.

Across Chesapeake Bay, on the Western Shore, lies Baltimore, one of the largest commercial and industrial cities in the country. Settled originally by members of the English upper class who preserved their customs for decades, Baltimore now has a large population of blue-collar workers, descendants of the many ethnic groups that migrated to the United States in the late 1800's and early 1900's.

The suburban counties of Maryland that border the District of Columbia form another distinct region. Expansion of the federal government has made this section of Maryland a center for military and civilian government installations.

And to the northwest, a narrow panhandle extends Maryland into the Appalachian hill country. The area acts as a haven for tourists, and many residents of this tri-state region identify with Pennsylvania and West Virginia as well as Delaware.

Each of Maryland's regions has its share of problems as well as assets. The rural Eastern Shore maintains a balance between agriculture and exurban development. Central Maryland, part of the corridor extending from Washington to Baltimore, is highly urbanized and thus increasingly plagued by problems common to cities. And the rural panhandle is a land of both tourism and poverty. But the regions also contain potential for development. Few states possess Maryland's cultural and economic variety with which to shape a future.

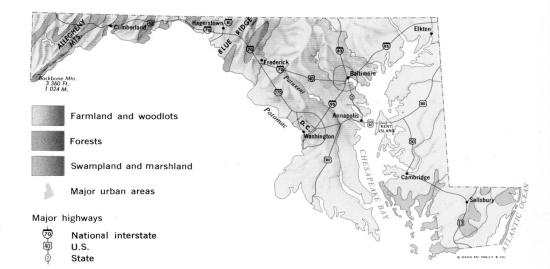

Farmland and woodlots

Forests

Swampland and marshland

Major urban areas

Major highways

National interstate

U.S.

State

Land Use Although most of Maryland's income comes from manufacturing, much of the state contains good farmland. Vegetables are grown on the Eastern Shore; tobacco is found in the southwest; and the Piedmont area is a productive dairy-farming region.

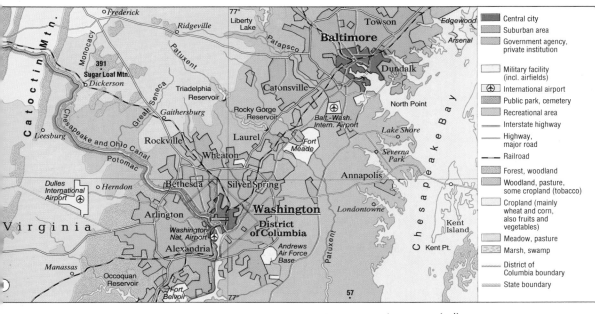

Central city

Suburban area

Government agency, private institution

Military facility (incl. airfields)

International airport

Public park, cemetery

Recreational area

Interstate highway

Highway, major road

Railroad

Forest, woodland

Woodland, pasture, some cropland (tobacco)

Cropland (mainly wheat and corn, also fruits and vegetables)

Meadow, pasture

Marsh, swamp

District of Columbia boundary

State boundary

Washington-Baltimore Corridor The concentration of transportation routes indicates Washington's and Baltimore's importance to each other and to the nation and the world.

Capital of Maryland and site of the United States Naval Academy, Annapolis played an important role in the early days of the United States. Today, the city retains a colonial atmosphere, with carefully preserved historical streets and buildings.

Washington, D.C.

POPULATION 623,300.
Density: 9,894 people/mi² (3,824 people/km²).*Urban:* 100%.
INCOME/CAPITA $16,908.
ESTABLISHED January, 1791.

CAPITAL Washington, 623,300.
LARGEST CITY Washington.
LAND AREA 63 mi² (163 km²).
DIMENSIONS N–S 15 miles, E–W 15 miles.

CLIMATE Hot, humid summers. Cool winters. Plentiful rainfall.

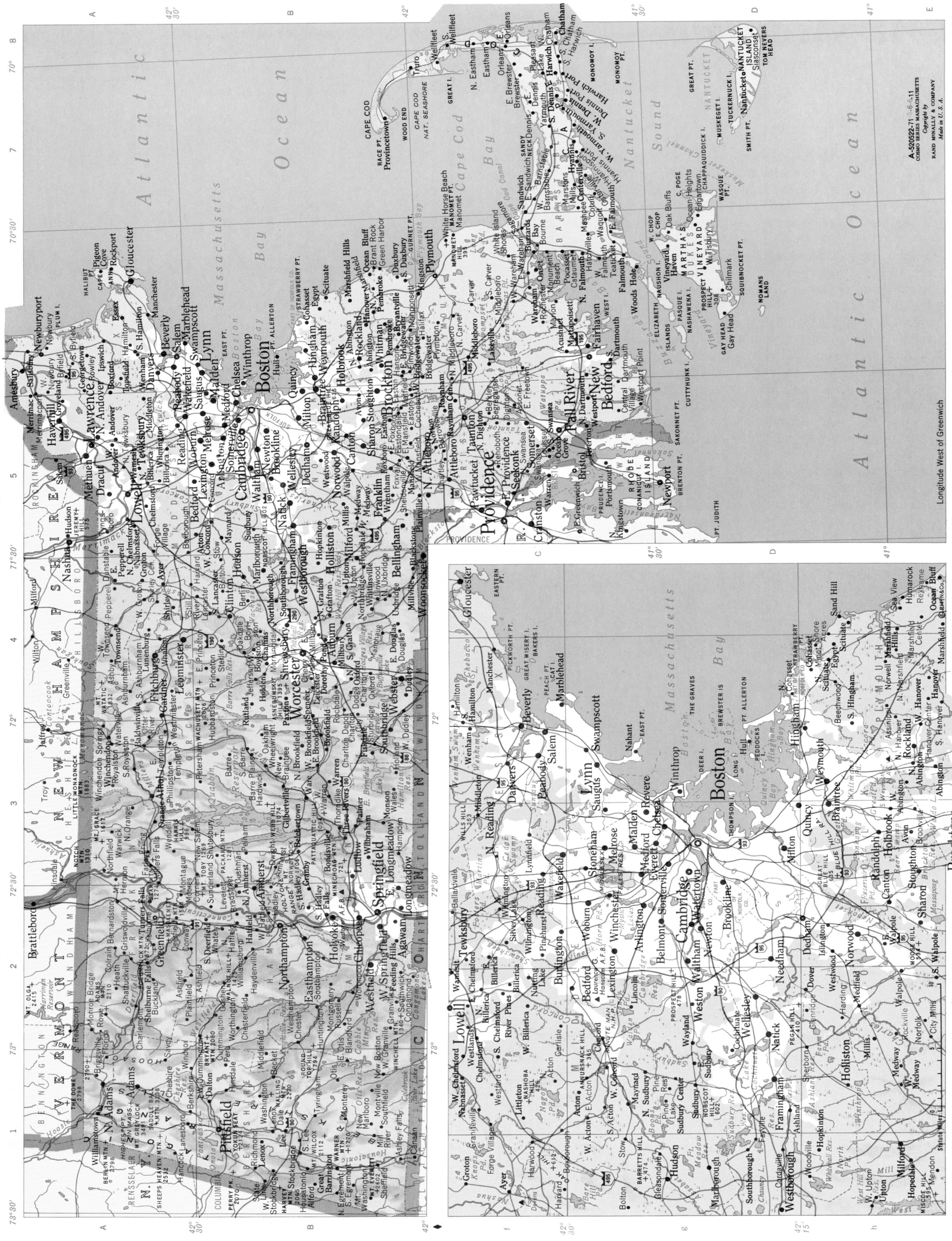

Cities and Towns*

Amherst 26,300 **B2**
Arlington 48,219 **B5**
Attleboro 34,196 **C5**
Belmont 26,100 **g11**
Beverly 37,655 **A6**
Boston 562,994 **B5**
Braintree 36,337 **B5**
Brockton 95,172 **B5**
Brookline 55,062 **B5**
Burlington 23,486 **f11**
Cambridge 95,322 **B5**
Chatham 1,922 **C8**
Chelmsford 31,174 **A5**
Chelsea 25,431 **B5**
Chicopee 55,112 **B2**
Concord 6,400 **B5**
Danvers 24,100 **A6**
Dedham 25,298 **B5**
Dracut 21,245 **A5**
Fall River 92,574 **C5**
Fitchburg 39,580 **A4**
Framingham 65,113 **B5**
Gloucester 27,768 **A6**
Great Barrington 3,150 **B1**
Greenfield 14,198 **A2**
Haverhill 46,865 **A5**
Holyoke 44,678 **B2**
Hyannis 8,000 **C7**
Lawrence 63,175 **A5**
Leominster 34,508 **A4**
Lexington 29,479 **B5**
Lowell 92,418 **A5**
Lynn 78,471 **B6**
Malden 53,386 **B5**
Marblehead 20,126 **B6**
Marlborough 30,617 **B4**
Medford 58,076 **B5**
Melrose 30,055 **B5**
Methuen 36,701 **A5**
Milford 23,390 **B4**
Milton 25,860 **B5**
Nantucket 3,229 **D7**
Natick 29,461 **B5**
Needham 27,901 **g11**
New Bedford 98,478 **C6**
Newburyport 15,900 **A6**
Newton 83,622 **B5**
North Adams 18,063 **A1**
Northampton 29,286 **B2**
North Attleboro 21,095 **C5**
Peabody 45,976 **A6**
Pittsfield 51,974 **B1**
Plymouth 7,232 **C6**
Provincetown 3,536 **B7**
Quincy 84,743 **B5**
Randolph 22,218 **B5**
Reading 22,678 **B5**
Revere 42,423 **g11**
Salem 38,220 **A6**
Somerville 77,372 **B5**
Southbridge 16,665 **B3**
Springfield 152,319 **B2**
Stoneham 21,424 **g11**
Stoughton 26,710 **B5**
Taunton 45,001 **C5**
Vineyard Haven 1,704 **D6**
Wakefield 24,895 **B5**
Waltham 58,200 **B5**
Watertown 34,384 **g11**
Wellesley 27,209 **B5**
Westfield 36,465 **B2**
West Springfield 27,042 **B2**
Weymouth 55,601 **B6**
Woburn 36,626 **B5**
Worcester 161,799 **B4**

*Populations are for localities, not incorporated towns.

Statute Miles
Kilometers

Lambert Conformal Conic Projection
SCALE 1:978,000   1 Inch = 15.5 Statute Miles

A-520522-71 · -6-6-11
COSMO SERIES MASSACHUSETTS
Copyright by
RAND McNALLY & COMPANY
Made in U. S. A.

Massachusetts

POPULATION 5,884,100.
Rank: 13.*Density:* 752 people/mi²
(290 people/km²).*Urban:*
83.8%.*Rural:* 16.2%.
INCOME/CAPITA $15,691.
Rank: 3.
ENTERED UNION Feb. 6, 1788,
6th state.

CAPITAL Boston, 566,900.
LARGEST CITY Boston.
LAND AREA 7,826 mi²
(20,269 km²).
Rank: 45.*Water area:* 460 mi²
(1,191 km²).
DIMENSIONS N–S 110 miles,
E–W 190 miles.

ELEVATIONS *Highest:* Mount
Greylock, 3,491 ft
(1,064 m).*Lowest:* Atlantic Ocean
shoreline, sea level.
CLIMATE Long, cold winters; warm
summers; moderate rainfall.

Boston is often called the Hub, a description that could easily apply to Massachusetts as a whole. Since the beginning of the country's history, social, cultural, and economic changes originating in this state have radiated outward to the rest of the nation.

In the 1600's, Massachusetts served as the mother colony for many settlements that spread throughout New England. In the late 1700's, sparks struck by Boston radicals helped ignite the Revolutionary War, leading the country into its battle for independence. Later, the Boston area became a pioneer of the Industrial Revolution and the development of mass production. Throughout the 1800's, thousands of immigrants poured into the state, moving first into the hub of Boston, then spreading outward to the north, south, and west.

Today, the state's sea routes, roads, and rivers not only cover New England but reach out to the nation and the world. Centered on the Boston area, these transport systems, like spokes of a wheel, extend in all directions and distribute goods and services to regional, national, and international markets.

The educational institutions in the state, such as the Massachusetts Institute of Technology, have also made Massachusetts a center for ideas and, most recently, a focal point for the electronics and communication industries. The area outside Boston represents one of the most important concentrations of research and development facilities in the United States. From here, inventions and ideas flow to other institutions and regions in the country.

Since World War II, however, much of American industry has shifted from the Northeast and Midwest to the South and West, and Massachusetts no longer plays as central a role as it once did. Nevertheless, the state shows its leadership in the development of industries in line with the nation's high-technology future. This leadership, combined with the state's experience and ingenuity in marketing and distributing innovations, will keep the Boston-Massachusetts hub turning for quite some time.

Cape Cod is made up mostly of sand and gravel deposited by glaciers. To ensure its preservation, the Cape Cod National Seashore was established along the Outer Cape. This is one of the few remaining natural regions of the Atlantic Coast, with its landscape of sand dunes, forests, heath, and ponds.

Education The state's investment in education, as evidenced by the large number of institutions, has paid off in a greater-than-average participation in higher education. The educational history of Massachusetts includes many "firsts"—from the colonies' first public school to the nation's first college, Harvard.

Massachusetts 116

United States 64
(average)

Massachusetts 303,800

United States 171,276
(average)

Number of Colleges
and Universities

Higher-Education
Enrollment

Land Use Whereas Massachusetts is fortunate that glaciers left the state with excellent harbors and landings, these ice sheets also stripped away much soil, leaving little fertile land. Despite the differing glacial inheritance of the state's coastal and inland areas, both express a beauty valued by residents and tourists alike.

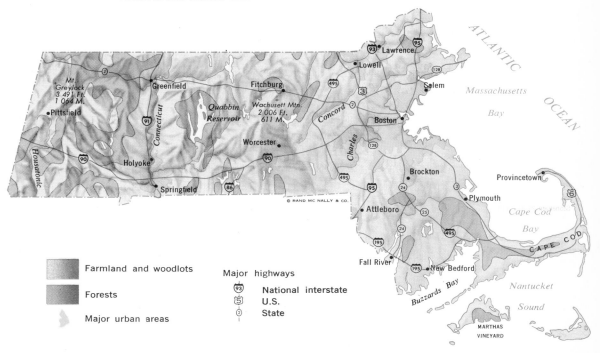

Farmland and woodlots

Forests

Major urban areas

Major highways
National interstate
U.S.
State

Cities and Towns*

Antrim 1,142 **D3**
Ashland 1,479 **C3**
Bedford 1,300 **E3**
Berlin 13,084 **B4**
Bristol 1,258 **C3**
Charlestown 1,294 **D2**
Claremont 14,557 **D2**
Colebrook 1,131 **g7**
Concord 30,400 **D3**
Contoocook 1,499 **D3**
Conway 1,781 **C4**
Derry 12,248 **E4**
Dover 22,377 **D5**
Durham 8,448 **D5**
Enfield 1,581 **C2**
Epping 1,384 **D4**
Exeter 8,947 **E5**
Farmington 3,284 **D4**
Franconia 600 **B3**
Franklin 7,901 **D3**
Goffstown 2,500 **D3**
Gorham 2,180 **B4**
Greenville 1,467 **E3**
Groveton 1,389 **A3**
Hampton 6,779 **E5**
Hanover 6,861 **C2**
Henniker 1,538 **D3**
Hillsboro 1,797 **D3**
Hinsdale 1,546 **E2**
Hooksett 1,868 **D4**
Hudson 6,248 **E4**
Jaffrey 2,684 **E2**
Keene 21,449 **E2**
Laconia 15,575 **C4**
Lancaster 2,134 **B3**
Lebanon 11,134 **C2**
Lincoln 950 **B3**
Lisbon 1,151 **B3**
Littleton 4,480 **B3**
Manchester 90,936 **E4**
Marlborough 1,231 **E2**
Meredith 1,202 **C3**
Merrimack 1,200 **E4**
Milford 6,289 **E3**
Milton 1,000 **D5**
Nashua 67,865 **E4**
New Castle 975 **D5**
New London 1,335 **D3**
Newmarket 3,749 **D5**
Newport 4,388 **D2**
North Conway 2,184 **B4**
Northfield 1,340 **D3**
North Hampton 1,000 **E5**
North Walpole 950 **D2**
Peterborough 2,100 **E3**
Pinardville 4,500 **E3**
Pittsfield 1,584 **D4**
Plaistow 1,800 **E4**
Plymouth 3,628 **C3**
Portsmouth 26,254 **D5**
Raymond 1,192 **D4**
Rochester 21,560 **D5**
Salem 11,500 **E4**
Somersworth 10,350 **D5**
South Hooksett 1,200 **D4**
Suncook 4,698 **D4**
Tilton 1,230 **D3**
Troy 1,318 **E2**
West Swanzey 1,022 **E2**
Whitefield 1,005 **B3**
Wilton 1,310 **E3**
Winchester 1,732 **E2**
Wolfeboro 2,000 **C4**
Woodsville 1,195 **B2**

*Populations are for localities, not incorporated towns.

New York

POPULATION 17,964,000.
Rank: 2.*Density:* 379 people/mi²
(146 people/km²).*Urban:*
84.6%.*Rural:* 15.4%.
INCOME/CAPITA $15,014.
Rank: 5.
ENTERED UNION July 26, 1788,
11th state.

CAPITAL Albany, 98,900.
LARGEST CITY New York,
7,304,300.
LAND AREA 47,379 mi²
(122,711 km²).
Rank: 30.*Water area:* 5,358 mi²
(13,877 km²)
DIMENSIONS N–S 310 miles,
E–W 330 miles.

ELEVATIONS *Highest:* Mount
Marcy, 5,344 ft (1,629 m).*Lowest:*
Atlantic Ocean shoreline, sea
level.
CLIMATE Cool winters, hot
summers in south. North and
west, cold winters, short
summers.

New York truly deserves its reputation as the Empire State. Its considerable influence extends from neighboring states to nations far beyond the shores of North America. As a result, New York City is more than America's largest urban area; in many ways it is the capital of the world's economy.

Yet surprisingly, New York State's economic potential was not realized until the nineteenth century, well after other colonial states had established a thriving commerce. New York's swift rise to fortune began with the settlement of the Great Lakes region and the upper Mississippi River valley. As these western territories grew, they found themselves separated from the markets and shipping routes of the East by the Appalachian Mountains. Because only New York had established river, canal, and rail routes through these mountains, the state quickly became the funnel through which foodstuffs, manufactured goods, and raw materials of the western regions poured into the East and beyond to overseas markets. The state not only served as the Midwest's gateway to the Atlantic, but rose to become North America's major port for world trade.

Today, New York is still a powerful presence in the nation. Its financial resources, evident in its bank holdings and stock exchanges, help to buffer the state during times of economic recession and industrial decline. No matter where in the United States a major factory or business is built, its owners are likely to turn to New York City for financing.

But New York's very size and strength has created special problems. As the capital of an economic empire, New York City attracts thousands of immigrants each year, many of whom are poor. The strain of assimilating so many newcomers adds to the city's already overburdened resources and, in turn, creates further tension between city and state administrators. Several times the federal government has been called in to help the city weather its financial crises. Longer-term solutions must be found if the city and state are to remain the symbol of what is best in the country. Because of the drive and energy of the people of New York, it is likely that the state will maintain its status as the capital of the empire.

The interdependence of New York's urban and rural areas is apparent in the state's agriculture. Heavily populated urban centers demand certain products, and New York's rural regions support their needs. The rich soils of the country's agricultural states are not to be found here, but much of the state's more productive land is intensively cultivated. Shown here, the Hudson Valley in southeastern New York provides dairy products and also ranks high in apple production.

Land Use New York's cities trace the important Atlantic-to-Great Lakes corridor that established the state's empire. These cities remain the home of most of the population and the site of major industries. Outside the cities lies farmland, and beyond this land are the recreation areas of the Appalachian Highlands, including the Catskills and the Adirondacks.

Farmland and woodlots

Forests

Livestock grazing (areas other than farmland)

Major urban areas

Major highways

National interstate

U.S.

State

Canal

Residential Areas

Low density (2 to 20 dwelling units per acre), mostly single-family homes and town houses with yards, also retail businesses and public and private institutions

Moderate-to-high density (20 to 90 dwelling units per acre), mostly multistory buildings and high rises, also retail businesses and public and private institutions

Highest density (90 to 275 dwelling units per acre), mostly high rises, retail businesses and public and private institutions

Major commercial center, mostly department stores and retail businesses

Central Business District, department stores, shops, public buildings (mostly skyscrapers)

Prominent skyscraper

University

Theater, concert hall, museum

U. N. mission, consulate

Hotel

Financial District, stock market, major bank, insurance company

Shopping area includes entertainment, nightclub district

Manufacturing and industrial area, warehouse, railroad yard

Urban-renewal area

Land-reclamation project

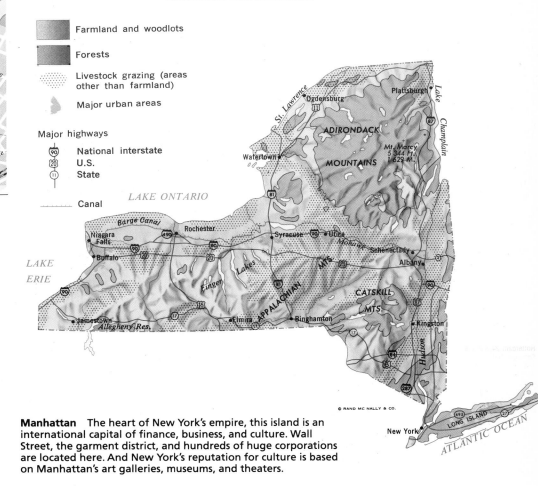

© RAND McNALLY & CO.

Manhattan The heart of New York's empire, this island is an international capital of finance, business, and culture. Wall Street, the garment district, and hundreds of huge corporations are located here. And New York's reputation for culture is based on Manhattan's art galleries, museums, and theaters.

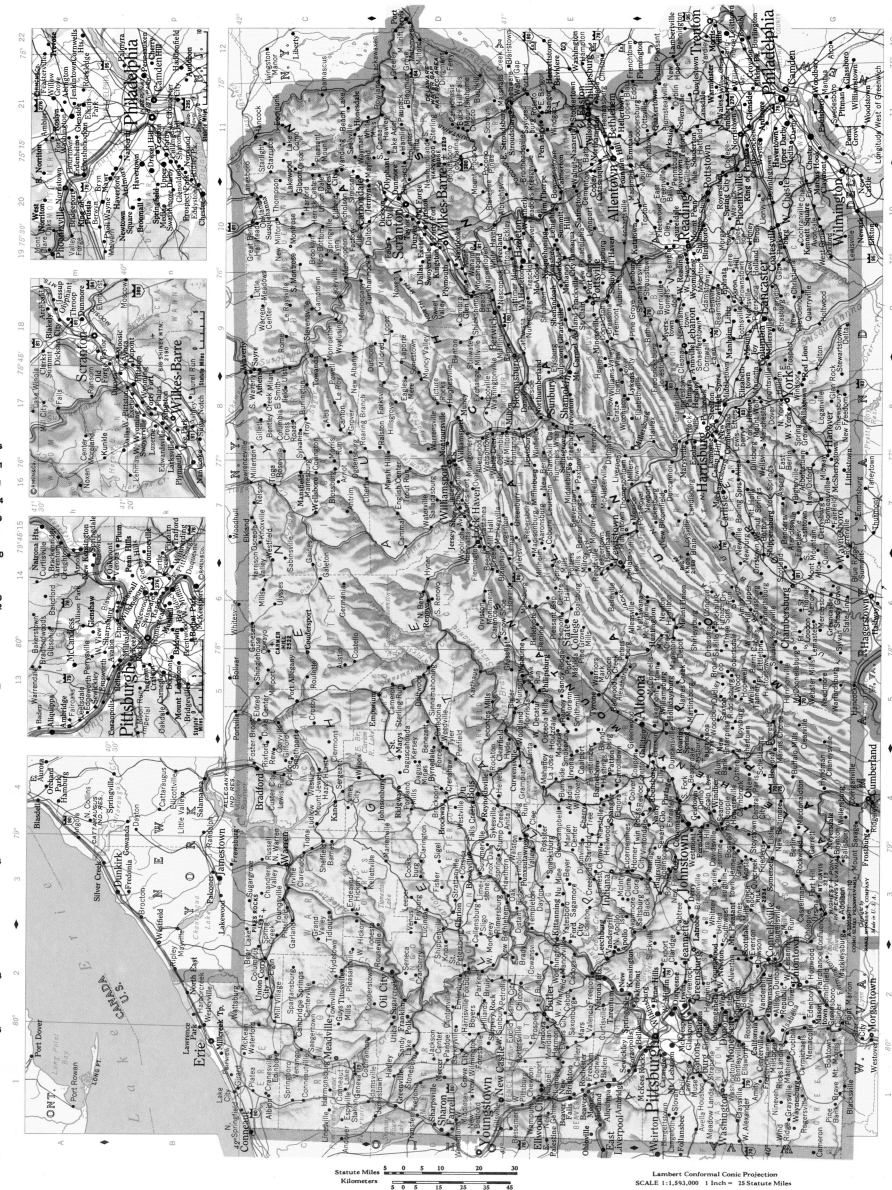

Cities and Towns

Aliquippa 17,094 **E1**
Allentown 103,758 **E11**
Altoona 57,078 **E5**
Beaver Falls 12,525 **E1**
Berwick 11,850 **D9**
Bethel Park 34,755 **k14**
Bethlehem 70,419 **E11**
Bloomsburg 11,717 **E9**
Bradford 11,211 **C4**
Broomall 23,642 **p20**
Butler 17,026 **E2**
Carbondale 11,255 **C10**
Carlisle 18,314 **F7**
Chambersburg 16,174 **G6**
Chester 45,794 **G11**
Coatesville 10,698 **G10**
Connellsville 10,319 **F2**
Du Bois 9,290 **D4**
Easton 26,027 **E11**
Ephrata 11,095 **F9**
Erie 119,123 **B1**
Gettysburg 7,194 **G7**
Greensburg 17,558 **F2**
Hanover 14,890 **G8**
Harrisburg 53,264 **F8**
Havertown 36,000 **G11**
Hazleton 27,318 **E10**
Hershey 9,000 **F8**
Indiana 16,051 **E3**
Jeannette 13,106 **F2**
Johnstown 35,496 **F4**
King of Prussia 18,200 **F11**
Lancaster 54,725 **F9**
Lansdale 16,526 **F11**
Latrobe 10,799 **F3**
Lebanon 25,711 **F9**
Levittown 78,600 **F12**
Lewistown 9,830 **E6**
Lock Haven 9,617 **D7**
McKeesport 31,012 **F2**
Meadville 15,544 **C1**
Middletown 10,122 **F8**
Millcreek Township 44,303 **B1**
Monroeville 30,977 **k14**
Mount Lebanon 34,414 **F1**
New Castle 33,621 **D1**
Norristown 34,684 **F11**
Oil City 13,881 **D2**
Penn Hills 57,632 **F2**
Philadelphia 1,688,210 **G11**
Pittsburgh 423,959 **F1**
Plum 25,390 **k14**
Pottstown 22,729 **F10**
Pottsville 18,195 **E9**
Punxsutawney 7,479 **E4**
Reading 78,686 **F10**
Scranton 88,117 **D10**
Shamokin 10,357 **E8**
Sharon 19,057 **D1**
Springfield 25,326 **p20**
State College 36,130 **E6**
Sunbury 12,292 **E8**
Uniontown 14,510 **G2**
Upper Darby 50,200 **G11**
Warminster 35,543 **F11**
Warren 12,146 **C3**
Washington 18,363 **F1**
Waynesboro 9,726 **G6**
West Chester 17,435 **G10**
West Mifflin 26,552 **F2**
Wilkes-Barre 51,551 **D10**
Wilkinsburg 23,669 **F2**
Williamsport 33,401 **D7**
Willow Grove 21,300 **F11**
York 44,619 **G8**

Statute Miles
Kilometers

Lambert Conformal Conic Projection
SCALE 1:1,593,000   1 Inch = 25 Statute Miles

Pennsylvania

POPULATION 11,973,400. *Rank:* 5.*Density:* 267 people/mi² (103 people/km²).*Urban:* 69.3%.*Rural:* 30.7%.
INCOME/CAPITA $12,940. *Rank:* 19.
ENTERED UNION Dec. 12, 1787, 2nd state.

CAPITAL Harrisburg, 52,100.
LARGEST CITY Philadelphia, 1,639,000.
LAND AREA 44,892 mi² (116,270 km²). *Rank:* 32.*Water area:* 1,155 mi² (2,991 km²).
DIMENSIONS N–S 180 miles, E–W 310 miles.

ELEVATIONS *Highest:* Mount Davis, 3,213 ft (979 m).*Lowest:* Along Delaware River, sea level.
CLIMATE Warm summers, cold winters; moderate rainfall, heavy snow in mountains.

Pennsylvania, the Keystone State, occupies its key location in two ways. First, it has long been the keystone in the north-south coastal arch formed by the original colonies. Second, it bridges the Appalachian Mountains between the coastal states and the vast interior lowland of America's midwestern heartland. These key roles are reflected in the character of its two largest cities.

Philadelphia, once the largest city in North America, played an important role in the Revolutionary War and in the unification of the colonies following independence; it remains the capstone of an entire era of American political and economic history. Although now a major port and part of the almost continuous urban-industrial belt extending along the northeastern seaboard, it is still sometimes called the Athens of America. In contrast, Pittsburgh is the "Steel City," and its factories are a monument to the industrialization of America in the nineteenth and twentieth centuries. Its resources and leadership were used to turn the East North Central states into an industrial powerhouse.

Despite their location in one state, Philadelphia in the east and Pittsburgh in the west exist in relative independence, with their own markets and spheres of influence. This independence developed in part because the Allegheny and Appalachian mountains long posed a barrier to east-west communications. Today, railroads and highways cross the state, but the effects of the division remain.

Nevertheless, the two cities have come to support the entire commonwealth, and their commerce and industry have been associated with a prosperous and diversified agriculture. Culturally, too, the state has displayed rich diversity, including groups such as the Amish, the Quakers, the Mennonites, the Appalachian Highlanders, the Eastern Europeans of the cities and mining towns, and the black communities of the largest cities.

Today, Pennsylvania remains a wealthy and important state. Well endowed with human and natural resources, it can be expected to play a key role in solving the problems it shares with its neighbors—high unemployment, the declining quality of the urban environment, ethnic and racial conflict, and other issues that confront the industrial northeastern United States.

Pennsylvania's farmlands and forests provide examples of environmental conservation. Unlike settlers elsewhere, early Pennsylvanian farmers practiced crop rotation, keeping the soil productive. Conservation of forests, however, came later. Rapid early development destroyed almost all of Pennsylvania's woodlands. At the end of the nineteenth century, conservation programs were enacted, restoring the forests that now cover over half the state. This south-central area near Kingwood consists of the rich farmland and forests that make up much of Pennsylvania.

Manufacturing Pennsylvania plays a key role in manufacturing, forming a major part of the industrial coastal megalopolis and linking it with the western portion of the nation's principal manufacturing region.

Number employed in manufacturing by county

- Over 100,000
- 50,000-100,000
- 20,000-50,000
- 10,000-20,000
- 2,000-10,000
- 0-2,000

Copyright © by Rand McNally & Co.

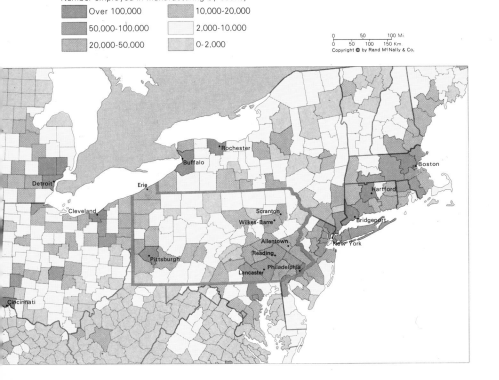

Land Use Pennsylvania's land patterns are shaped by the Appalachian Mountains and the Allegheny Plateau. Forests generally follow the mountain crests, outlining a natural maze, while urban industrialized areas and agricultural activities fill the valleys in a complex but effective mix.

- Farmland and woodlots
- Forests
- Major urban areas
- Major highways
- 80 National interstate
- 6 U.S.

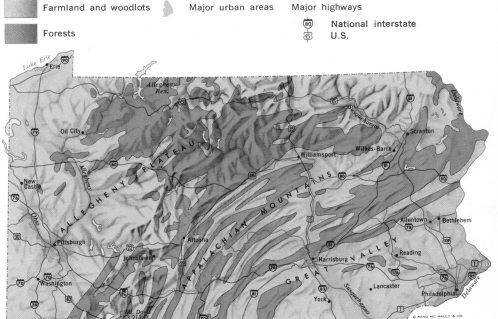

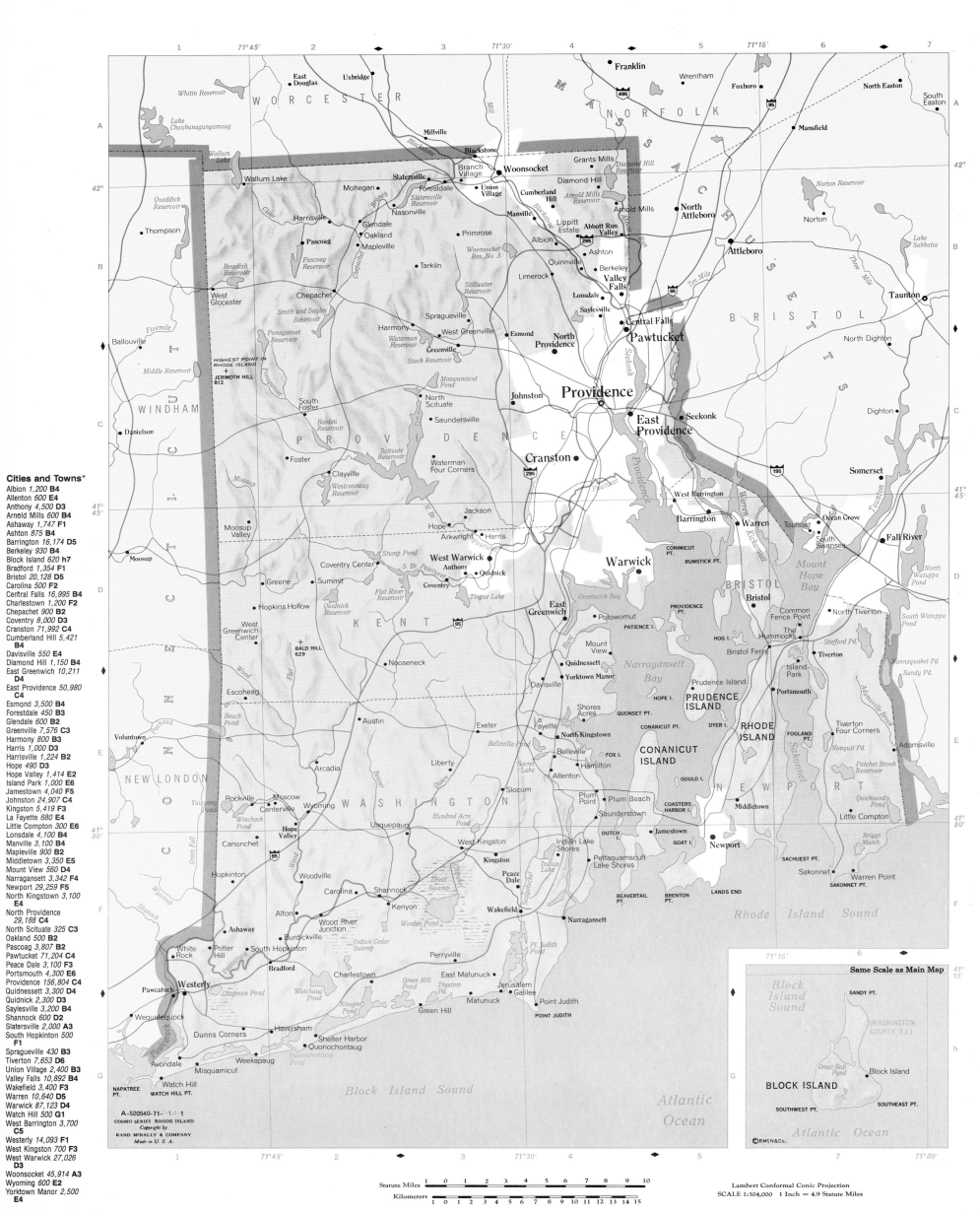

Cities and Towns*

Albion 1,200 **B4**
Allenton 600 **E4**
Anthony 4,500 **D3**
Arnold Mills 600 **B4**
Ashaway 1,747 **F1**
Ashton 875 **B4**
Barrington 16,174 **D5**
Berkeley 930 **B4**
Block Island 620 **h7**
Bradford 1,354 **F1**
Bristol 20,128 **D5**
Carolina 500 **F2**
Central Falls 16,995 **B4**
Charlestown 1,200 **F2**
Chepachet 900 **B2**
Coventry 8,000 **D3**
Cranston 71,992 **C4**
Cumberland Hill 5,421 **B4**
Davisville 550 **E4**
Diamond Hill 1,150 **B4**
East Greenwich 10,211 **D4**
East Providence 50,980 **C4**
Esmond 3,500 **B4**
Forestdale 450 **B3**
Glendale 600 **B2**
Greenville 7,576 **C3**
Harmony 800 **B3**
Harris 1,000 **D3**
Harrisville 1,224 **B2**
Hope 490 **D3**
Hope Valley 1,414 **E2**
Island Park 1,000 **E6**
Jamestown 4,040 **F5**
Johnston 24,907 **C4**
Kingston 5,419 **F3**
La Fayette 680 **E4**
Little Compton 300 **E6**
Lonsdale 4,100 **B4**
Manville 3,100 **B4**
Mapleville 900 **B2**
Middletown 3,350 **E5**
Mount View 560 **D4**
Narragansett 3,342 **F4**
Newport 29,259 **F5**
North Kingstown 3,100 **E4**
North Providence 29,188 **C4**
North Scituate 325 **C3**
Oakland 500 **B2**
Pascoag 3,807 **B2**
Pawtucket 71,204 **C4**
Peace Dale 3,100 **F3**
Portsmouth 4,300 **E6**
Providence 156,804 **C4**
Quidnessett 3,300 **D4**
Quidnick 2,300 **D3**
Saylesville 3,200 **B4**
Shannock 600 **D2**
Slatersville 2,000 **A3**
South Hopkinton 500 **F1**
Spragueville 430 **B3**
Tiverton 7,653 **D6**
Union Village 2,400 **B3**
Valley Falls 10,892 **B4**
Wakefield 3,400 **F3**
Warren 10,640 **D5**
Warwick 87,123 **D4**
Watch Hill 500 **G1**
West Barrington 3,700 **C5**
Westerly 14,093 **F1**
West Kingston 700 **F3**
West Warwick 27,026 **D3**
Woonsocket 45,914 **A3**
Wyoming 600 **E2**
Yorktown Manor 2,500 **E4**

*Populations are for localities, not incorporated towns.

Statute Miles 1 0 1 2 3 4 5 6 7 8 9 10
Kilometers 1 0 1 2 3 4 5 6 7 8 9 10 11 12 13 14 15

A-520540-71- -1-1-1
COSMO SERIES RHODE ISLAND
Copyright by
RAND MCNALLY & COMPANY
Made in U.S.A.

Lambert Conformal Conic Projection
SCALE 1:304,000   1 Inch = 4.9 Statute Miles

Same Scale as Main Map

BLOCK ISLAND
(WASHINGTON COUNTY, R.I.)

Top– ROCK BRIDGE, RED RIVER GORGE / KENTUCKY

Bottom– NATURAL BRIDGE / ALABAMA

SPANISH MOSS ALONG SOUTH RIVER / NORTH CAROLINA

RHODODENDRONS ON MT. MITCHELL, BLUE RIDGE PARKWAY / NORTH CAROLINA

Left– NEW RIVER GORGE, GRANDVIEW STATE PARK / WEST VIRGINIA

Right– CEDAR ON LEDGE RIM, MAGAZINE MOUNTAIN / ARKANSAS

Left– CUMBERLAND FALLS STATE PARK / KENTUCKY

Below– DOGWOOD, TABLE ROCK STATE PARK / SOUTH CAROLINA

Top– PINNACLE OVERLOOK, CUMBERLAND GAP NATIONAL
HISTORIC PARK / TENNESSEE-KENTUCKY-VIRGINIA

Bottom– CASH LAKE, DESOTO STATE PARK / ALABAMA

Left– NATIVE GRASSES, PEA RIDGE NATIONAL MILITARY PARK / ARKANSAS

Above– SEA OATS, SANIBEL ISLAND / FLORIDA

Left– COCO PALMS, KEY WEST / FLORIDA

Right– POND CYPRESS AND LILY PADS, COOKS HAMMOCK / FLORIDA

Maps of the South

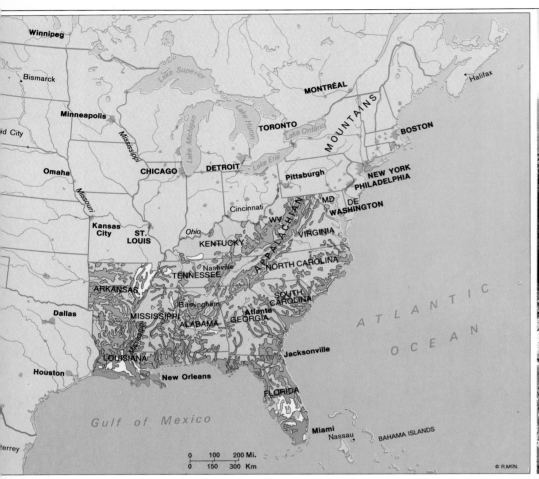

Land Use Swamps and forests edge the extensive coastline of the Southeast, extending inland along rivers that penetrate the rolling terrain of the interior. Farmland with woodlots characterize many inner regions, although rich, almost treeless expanses of agricultural land can be found—especially along the Mississippi River. Large expanses of forests occupy the steeper slopes and higher elevations of the Appalachian Mountains.

The Appalachians cover much of the Southeast from West Virginia to Alabama. Parallel northeast-to-southwest mountains and valleys have influenced transportation, with east-west communication routes funneled through valleys and relatively few gaps in the terrain. Settlement and cultivation, too, are restricted to valleys. But at the same time, the mountains contribute an abundant mineral and forest resource and great natural beauty for a growing tourist trade. The picture shows a typical ridge-and-valley area near Spruce Knob in West Virginia.

Few regions have drawn their legends and heroes in such fine detail as has the Southeast. With the cultural inheritance of the Old South, these states evoke images of a life-style and landscape as unique and vivid as those cherished by the Yankees of New England. Although the region's tradition suggests an origin of common heritage, the rich imagery of the Southeast springs from the diversity of its land and people more than from their similarity. The region may lack the geographic extremes of rugged mountain and desert, but here is just as dramatic a cultural landscape.

The Southeast expresses a pattern, set long before the Civil War, that differentiates between the upland and lowland South. The former is a region of small farms; the latter was originally dedicated to plantation agriculture. These two different regions are splintered even further. The lowlands are composed of the Atlantic Sea Islands, the Coastal Lowland, and the Piedmont. Waves of settlers emanating from the East, the North, and the Gulf Coast swept across the region to compound cultural fragmentation. A community's distance from coastal-area cities—such as Baltimore, Richmond, Wilmington, Charleston, and New Orleans—often accentuated existing differences. Discord was more common than harmony; upland farmers often allied themselves politically against the lowland planters.

The Southeast still reflects the strain of its cultural fragmentation, especially at its geographic extremes. Florida contrasts so sharply with the rest of the Southeast in character and demography that it could almost belong to a different region. Parts of Maryland and Virginia are included in America's northeastern megalopolis, and both these states are tied to the national government in Washington, D.C.

These differences make it difficult to generalize about population growth and change in the Southeast. Even patterns of migration into, around, and out of the region are complicated. As a consequence, while the area is growing in population, the age, racial, and educational profiles of its states are changing at different rates. Rural blacks tend to leave the region or move to its cities, and their white counterparts remain in the region, also moving primarily to its cities. Retirees and vacationers continue to seek out inland areas, such as the Arkansas Ozarks, and Atlantic and Gulf Coast communities. Meanwhile, cities such as Miami and Tampa have attracted immigrants from Caribbean nations; and other rapidly growing cities, exemplified by Atlanta, now draw northern business people and professionals in large numbers. Manufacturing and construction industries also more frequently attract workers from the North.

Forecasting the region's economic future is similarly problematic. The industrial accomplishments of certain Southeast states rival those of their northern counterparts. Activities such as the production of chemicals are found in the factories of Delaware and in the plants of the Louisiana-Texas Gulf Coast.

Low literacy rates, rural poverty, and other barriers to economic progress are being overcome. The Southeast is also overcoming its prolonged reliance on agriculture and its general failure of the past to build a manufacturing base commensurate with its size. However, this one-time drawback can act as an asset. Unencumbered by a large amount of heavy industry, the Southeast is in an excellent position to diversify into today's light and high-technology industries.

In truth, there are many Southeasts, reflecting the traditional difference between upland and lowland and the unique way each state's economy is diversifying. States such as Georgia have launched themselves into the mainstream of current American economic trends; others, such as Florida, have been sought out by the rest of the nation. Thus, behind the evocative images of the Old South lie many New Souths, and the features of each are early in the making.

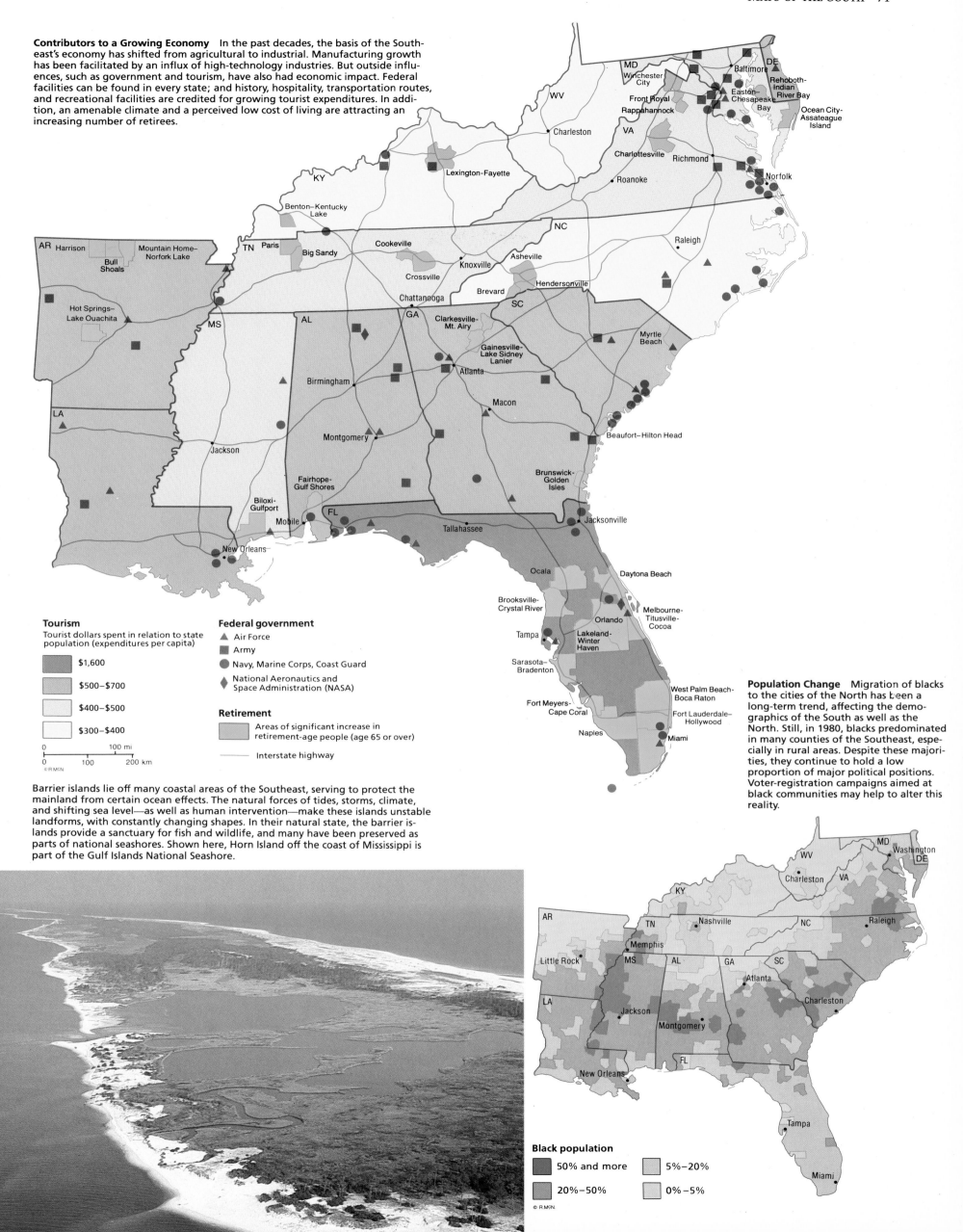

Contributors to a Growing Economy In the past decades, the basis of the Southeast's economy has shifted from agricultural to industrial. Manufacturing growth has been facilitated by an influx of high-technology industries. But outside influences, such as government and tourism, have also had economic impact. Federal facilities can be found in every state; and history, hospitality, transportation routes, and recreational facilities are credited for growing tourist expenditures. In addition, an amenable climate and a perceived low cost of living are attracting an increasing number of retirees.

Tourism
Tourist dollars spent in relation to state population (expenditures per capita)

$1,600
$500–$700
$400–$500
$300–$400

0   100 mi
0   100   200 km
© R.MᶜN.

Federal government
▲ Air Force
■ Army
● Navy, Marine Corps, Coast Guard
♦ National Aeronautics and Space Administration (NASA)

Retirement
Areas of significant increase in retirement-age people (age 65 or over)
— Interstate highway

Barrier islands lie off many coastal areas of the Southeast, serving to protect the mainland from certain ocean effects. The natural forces of tides, storms, climate, and shifting sea level—as well as human intervention—make these islands unstable landforms, with constantly changing shapes. In their natural state, the barrier islands provide a sanctuary for fish and wildlife, and many have been preserved as parts of national seashores. Shown here, Horn Island off the coast of Mississippi is part of the Gulf Islands National Seashore.

Population Change Migration of blacks to the cities of the North has been a long-term trend, affecting the demographics of the South as well as the North. Still, in 1980, blacks predominated in many counties of the Southeast, especially in rural areas. Despite these majorities, they continue to hold a low proportion of major political positions. Voter-registration campaigns aimed at black communities may help to alter this reality.

Black population
50% and more
20%–50%
5%–20%
0%–5%
© R.MᶜN.

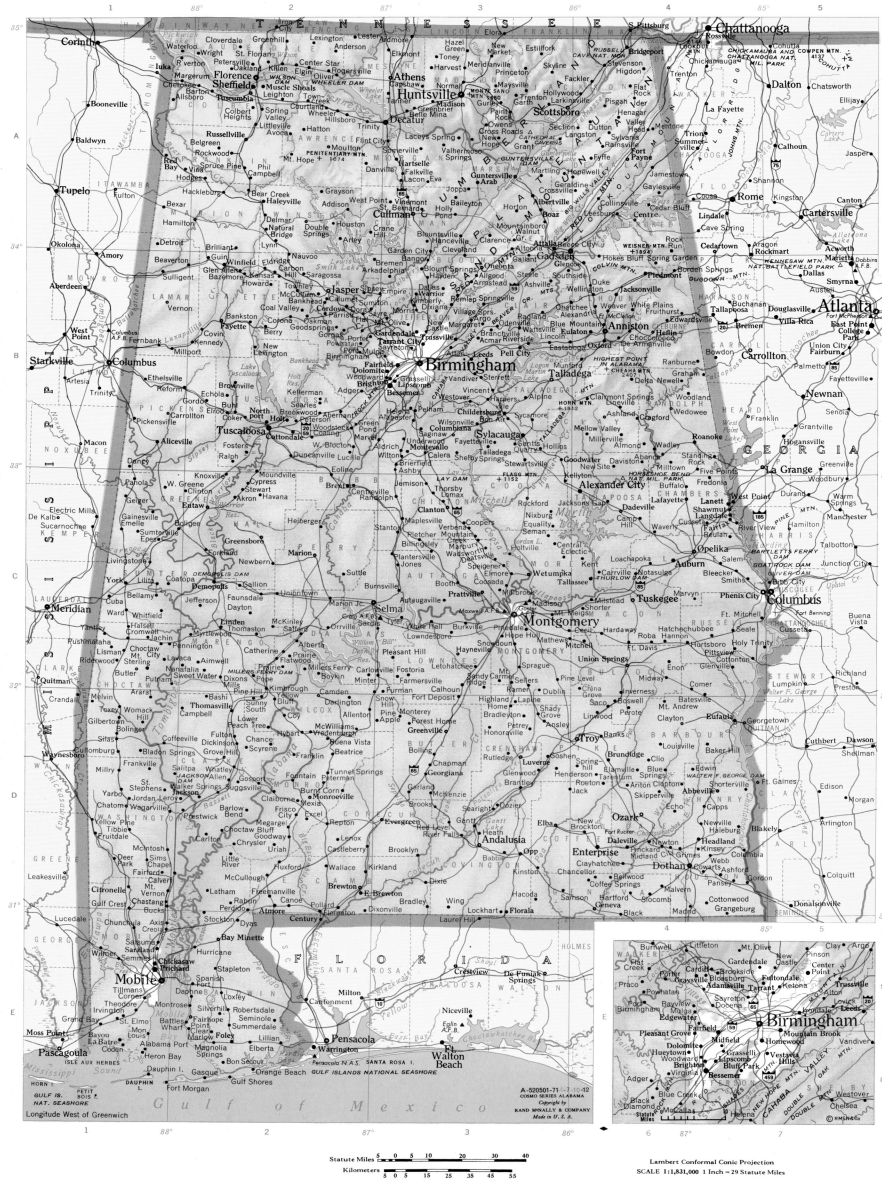

Cities and Towns

Albertville 12,039 A3
Alexander City 13,807 C4
Andalusia 10,415 D3
Anniston 29,523 B4
Arab 5,967 A3
Athens 14,558 A3
Atmore 8,789 D2
Auburn 28,471 C4
Bay Minette 7,455 E2
Bessemer 31,729 B3
Birmingham 286,799 B3
Bluff Park 12,000 g7
Boaz 7,151 A3
Brewton 6,680 D2
Center Point 23,317 f7
Childersburg 5,034 B3
Clanton 5,832 C3
Cullman 13,084 A3
Decatur 42,002 A3
Demopolis 7,678 C2
Dothan 48,750 D4
Enterprise 18,033 D4
Eufaula 12,097 D4
Fairfield 13,242 B3
Fayette 5,287 B2
Florence 37,029 A2
Fort Payne 11,485 A4
Gadsden 47,565 A3
Geneva 4,866 D4
Greenville 7,807 D3
Guntersville 7,041 A3
Haleyville 5,306 A2
Hamilton 5,093 A2
Hartselle 8,858 A3
Homewood 21,412 g7
Hueytown 13,478 g6
Huntsville 142,513 A3
Jackson 6,073 D2
Jacksonville 9,735 B4
Jasper 11,894 B2
Lanett 6,897 C4
Leeds 8,638 B3
Mobile 200,452 E1
Monroeville 5,674 D2
Montgomery 177,857 C3
Moundville 1,310 C2
Mountain Brook 19,718 g7
Muscle Shoals 8,911 A2
Northport 14,291 B2
Opelika 21,896 C4
Opp 7,204 D3
Ozark 13,188 D4
Pell City 6,616 B3
Phenix City 26,928 C4
Piedmont 5,544 B4
Prattville 18,647 C3
Prichard 39,541 E1
Roanoke 5,896 B4
Russellville 8,195 A2
Saraland 9,833 E1
Scottsboro 14,758 A3
Selma 26,684 C2
Sheffield 11,903 A2
Spanish Fort 3,415 E2
Sylacauga 12,708 B3
Talladega 19,128 B3
Tallassee 4,763 C4
Troy 12,945 D4
Tuscaloosa 75,211 B2
Tuscumbia 9,137 A2
Tuskegee 13,327 C4
Vestavia Hills 15,722 g7
Warrior 3,260 B3
Wetumpka 4,341 C3

Statute Miles   5 0 5 10   20   30   40
Kilometers   5 0 5 15   30   45   55

A-520501-71- -7-10-12
COSMO SERIES ALABAMA
Copyright by
RAND MCNALLY & COMPANY
Made in U. S. A.

Lambert Conformal Conic Projection
SCALE 1:1,831,000 1 Inch = 29 Statute Miles

© RMCN & Co

Alabama

POPULATION 4,137,100.
Rank: 22.*Density:* 81 people/mi²
(31 people/km²).*Urban:*
60.0%.*Rural:* 40.0%.
INCOME/CAPITA $9,907.
Rank: 47.
ENTERED UNION Dec. 14, 1819,
22nd state.

CAPITAL Montgomery, 196,500.
LARGEST CITY Birmingham,
280,900.
LAND AREA 50,766 mi²
(131,483 km²).
Rank: 28.*Water area:* 938 mi²
(2,429 km²).
DIMENSIONS N–S 330 miles,
E–W 200 miles.

ELEVATIONS *Highest:* Cheaha
Mountain, 2,407 ft
(734 m).*Lowest:* Gulf of Mexico
shoreline, sea level.
CLIMATE Humid with long, hot
summers; short, mild winters.
Long growing season, heavy
rainfall.

In heavy industry, Alabama is a powerhouse of the Deep South. Its principal manufacturing city, Birmingham, is sometimes called the Pittsburgh of the South. Alabama is often held up as an example of how the agricultural South of the past is changing into a new industrial region, better integrated into the national trend away from farming and toward industry.

Like many other southern states, Alabama once depended on a single crop, cotton, as the basis for its economy. Fortunately, deposits of iron ore, coal, and limestone—rarely found together in a single southern state—helped spur development of heavy manufacturing. Thus, even though cotton remains an important crop, Alabama has diversified into sectors that other states lacked the resources to enter.

Today, Alabama's coal and oil not only power the steel mills and metal-fabrication plants near Birmingham but also fuel its petrochemical and plastics industries. Linked northward to Tennessee's TVA-inspired industrialization and southward to the manufacturing growth along the Gulf of Mexico from Florida to Texas, Alabama is in a position to tap two sources of development and change. This potential should not be underestimated, for Alabama is also well equipped with transportation systems that can support new growth. These systems include waterways, railroads, and the modern seaport of Mobile.

However, Alabama's progress has not been solely in the industrial sector. The state's one-crop agriculture has also diversified in ways that serve to stabilize the economy. Alabama has reforested timberland to ensure lumber harvests in the future. Dairy farming, poultry and cattle raising, and soybean production have all increased substantially and contribute to national as well as regional markets. Moreover, Alabama's race relations have improved since the days when Martin Luther King focused national attention on racial problems.

However, the shift to a prosperous industrial economy supplemented by agriculture is not complete. As elsewhere in the South, per capita income is relatively low, and much of the population lives in rural areas. Yet, while Alabama is still in a state of transition, the outlines of a successful future have been established.

Alabama's natural resources are not confined to its land area. Like many other Gulf Coast states, Alabama contains offshore natural-gas deposits. Rising gas production is a result of recent drilling operations taking place at the mouth of Mobile Bay and other areas.

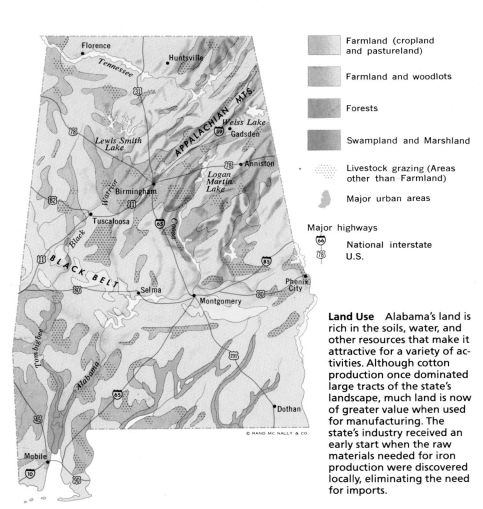

Farmland (cropland and pastureland)

Farmland and woodlots

Forests

Swampland and Marshland

Livestock grazing (Areas other than Farmland)

Major urban areas

Major highways
National interstate
U.S.

Major forest types

Longleaf pine, slash pine

Loblolly pine, shortleaf pine

Oak, pine

Oak, hickory

Oak, gum, cypress

Less than 10% forest

Land Use Alabama's land is rich in the soils, water, and other resources that make it attractive for a variety of activities. Although cotton production once dominated large tracts of the state's landscape, much land is now of greater value when used for manufacturing. The state's industry received an early start when the raw materials needed for iron production were discovered locally, eliminating the need for imports.

Southern Forests Almost two-thirds of Alabama's land is covered with forests, and these constitute an important natural resource for the state. Most of this forest area is used for private commercial enterprises; thus, forestry is one of Alabama's major industries. Lumbering in the state depends upon the widespread pine forests, which contain loblolly, shortleaf, slash, and other pines that are common throughout the Southeast. Over the past decades, conservation practices have been introduced to ensure the future success of activities based upon this resource.

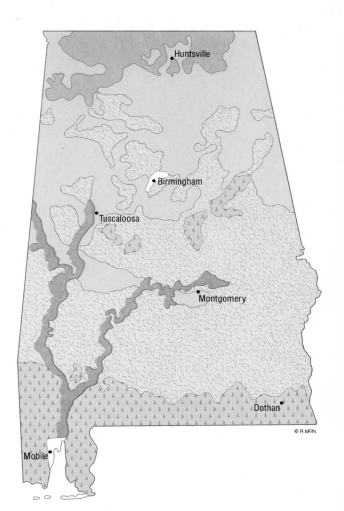

Cities and Towns

Statute Miles 5 0 5 10 20 30 40
Kilometers 5 0 5 15 25 35 45 55

Lambert Conformal Conic Projection
SCALE 1:1,832,000 1 Inch = 29 Statute Miles

Arkansas

POPULATION 2,420,000.
Rank: 33.*Density:* 46 people/mi²
(18 people/km²).*Urban:*
51.6%.*Rural:* 48.4%.
INCOME/CAPITA $10,142.
Rank: 42.
ENTERED UNION June 15, 1836,
25th state.

CAPITAL Little Rock, 190,000.
LARGEST CITY Little Rock.
LAND AREA 52,082 mi²
(134,892 km²).
Rank: 27.*Water area:* 1,109 mi²
(2,872 km²).
DIMENSIONS N–S 240 miles,
E–W 275 miles.

ELEVATIONS *Highest:* Magazine
Mountain, 2,753 ft
(839 m).*Lowest:* Along Ouachita
River,
55 ft (17 m).
CLIMATE Moderately long, hot
summers; short, mild winters.
Abundant rainfall.

Over the past two decades, Arkansas has been recharting its course in order to meet the future. For much of its history, Arkansas was a one-crop state, dominated by cotton. The focus on one crop meant that other resources remained undeveloped.

For generations, however, Arkansas had little reason to change. Cotton was a lucrative business in the south and east regions; and cotton growers, shippers, and manufacturers could easily wrest political control of the state from farmers living in the forested uplands to the north and west. The only early pretender to cotton's throne arose from the development of Arkansas's vast bauxite deposits, which still account for much of the total United States supply. In time, however, the people came to realize that their land could be put to more productive use.

Today, Arkansas's fortunes are changing. King Cotton has been deposed, and Arkansas is at last putting to use the full range of its natural and human resources. Soybeans, poultry, and rice share the limelight with cotton in the state's diversified agriculture. The production of oil, gas, and coal has boosted the state's revenues. Pine and hardwood forests, blanketing about half the state, supply timber for furniture and wood products. Arkansas's mineral waters, believed to be beneficial in treating certain illnesses, and the scenic beauty of the Ozark Mountains attract thousands of tourists and retirees each year. And as a state that once caused controversy in its opposition to school desegregation, Arkansas has since worked hard to build a more pluralistic, balanced society.

These changes have resulted in a dramatic rise in the state's per capita income, and its population, once tied to the land, is now concentrated in the cities, reflecting the pattern of urban growth experienced in other states. Moving from a one-crop state to a thriving, highly diversified region, Arkansas has chosen a new direction for itself, one that sets it firmly on the road to the future.

Unlike most crops, lowland rice grows best when its roots are submerged in water, and flooding a rice field also eliminates weeds. Arkansas's lowlands are especially suitable for rice production; the state provides much of the nation's supply.

Land Use In the northern and western uplands of the Ouachita and Ozark mountains, livestock, hay, fruit, and vegetable production is common. On the southern and eastern lowlands, soils support a still broader variety of cash and staple crops.

- Farmland (cropland and pastureland)
- Farmland and woodlots
- Forests
- Swampland and marshland
- Irrigated areas

- Livestock grazing (areas other than farmland)
- Major urban areas

Major Highways
- 15 National interstate
- 13 U.S.

Water Transport The Arkansas River navigation system enables ships to travel from the Mississippi River all the way to Tulsa, Oklahoma. By connecting with the Mississippi River—Gulf of Mexico intercoastal waterway, the system makes Arkansas an integral part of United States water transport, with ports along the Arkansas River accessible to international trade.

Elevation, in feet
- 2,000 or more
- 1,000–2,000
- 500–1,000
- 150–500
- 0–150
- Lock, dam, or lock and dam

Arkansas River navigation, in miles
500 450 400 350 300 250 200 150 100 50 0

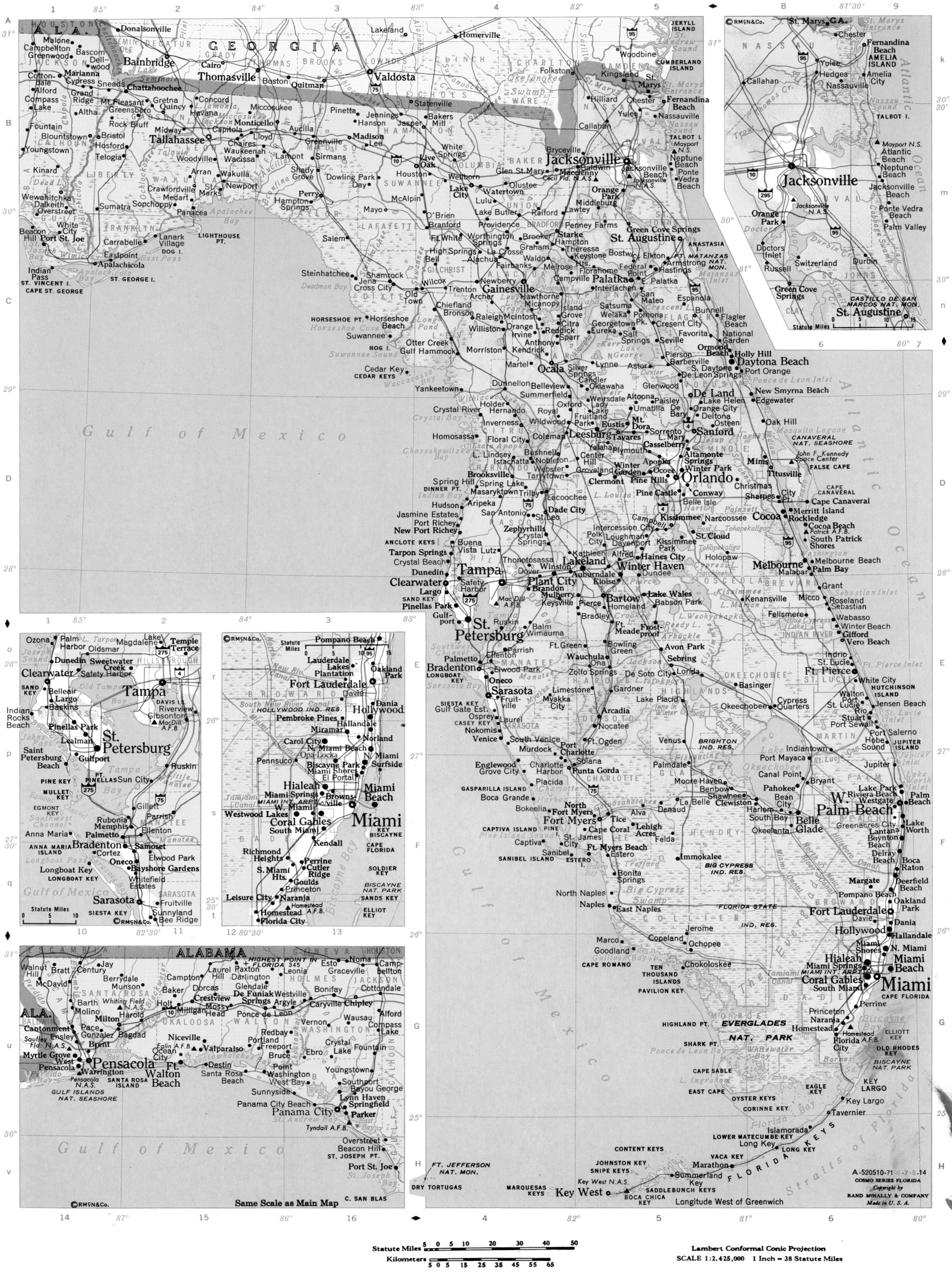

Cities and Towns

Bartow 14,780 **E5**
Belle Glade 16,535 **F6**
Boca Raton 49,505 **F6**
Boynton Beach 35,624 **F6**
Bradenton 30,170 **E4**
Brandon 29,100 **E4**
Cape Canaveral 5,733 **D6**
Cape Coral 32,103 **F5**
Carol City 47,349 **s13**
Clearwater 85,528 **E4**
Cocoa 16,096 **D6**
Coral Gables 43,241 **G6**
Daytona Beach 54,176 **C5**
Deerfield Beach 39,193 **F6**
De Land 15,354 **C5**
Delray Beach 34,325 **F6**
Dunedin 30,203 **D4**
Fort Lauderdale 153,279 **F6**
Fort Myers 36,638 **F5**
Fort Pierce 33,802 **E6**
Fort Walton Beach 20,829 **u15**
Gainesville 81,371 **C4**
Hallandale 36,517 **G6**
Hialeah 145,254 **G6**
Hollywood 121,323 **F6**
Homestead 20,668 **G6**
Immokalee 11,038 **F5**
Jacksonville 540,920 **B5**
Kendall 51,000 **s13**
Key Largo 7,447 **G6**
Key West 24,382 **H5**
Kissimmee 15,487 **D5**
Lake City 9,257 **B4**
Lakeland 47,406 **D5**
Lake Worth 27,048 **F6**
Largo 58,977 **E4**
Leesburg 13,191 **D5**
Marathon 7,508 **H5**
Margate 35,900 **F6**
Melbourne 46,536 **D6**
Merritt Island 30,708 **D6**
Miami 346,865 **G6**
Miami Beach 96,298 **G6**
Miramar 32,813 **s13**
Naples 17,581 **F5**
New Smyrna Beach 13,557 **C6**
North Miami 36,553 **G6**
North Miami Beach 36,481 **s13**
Ocala 37,170 **C4**
Orlando 128,291 **D5**
Panama City 33,346 **u16**
Pembroke Pines 35,776 **r13**
Pensacola 57,619 **u14**
Pinellas Park 32,811 **E4**
Plantation 48,653 **r13**
Plant City 17,064 **D4**
Pompano Beach 52,618 **F6**
Port Charlotte 25,770 **F4**
Riviera Beach 26,489 **F6**
St. Augustine 11,985 **C5**
St. Petersburg 238,647 **E4**
Sanford 23,176 **D5**
Sarasota 48,868 **E4**
Sebring 8,736 **E5**
Tallahassee 81,548 **B2**
Tampa 271,523 **E4**
Tarpon Springs 13,251 **D4**
Titusville 31,910 **D6**
Venice 12,153 **E4**
Vero Beach 16,176 **E6**
West Palm Beach 63,305 **F6**
West Pensacola 24,571 **u14**
Winter Haven 21,119 **D5**

Statute Miles 5 0 10 20 30 40 50
Kilometers 5 0 5 15 25 35 45 65

Lambert Conformal Conic Projection
SCALE 1:2,425,000 1 Inch = 38 Statute Miles

Same Scale as Main Map

A-520510-71 ——7-5-14
COSMO SERIES FLORIDA
Copyright by
RAND MNALLY & COMPANY
Made in U.S.A.

Longitude West of Greenwich

Florida

POPULATION 12,163,900.
Rank: 4.*Density:* 225 people/mi²
(87 people/km²).*Urban:*
84.3%.*Rural:* 15.7%.
INCOME/CAPITA $12,911.
Rank: 20.
ENTERED UNION March 3, 1845,
27th state.

CAPITAL Tallahassee, 125,000.
LARGEST CITY Jacksonville,
634,600.
LAND AREA 54,157 mi²
(140,266 km²).
Rank: 26.*Water area:* 4,511 mi²
(11,683 km²)
DIMENSIONS N–S 460 miles,
E–W 400 miles.

ELEVATIONS *Highest:* In Walton
County, 345 ft (105 m).*Lowest:*
Atlantic Ocean shoreline, sea
level.
CLIMATE Hot, humid summers;
mild winters. Heavy rains during
hurricane season.

Few states can challenge Florida's claim as the vacation and retirement capital of the country. It is a virtual melting pot of tourists, retirees, native residents, and immigrants from other states
and nations. In this regard, it is the most "northern" of the states in
the South.

Though Florida lies in the hurricane belt, its subtropical weather
more than makes up for these occasional storms. Warm, sunlit fall and
winter months attract the tourist trade from November to late March.
Miles of glistening beaches border the peninsula, and marshland has
given way to theme parks and the glitter of Miami and other coastal
towns. The warm weather also brings those who come to stay—
wealthy residents and retirees from the North and Midwest. Businesses, too, have followed the general migration to Florida's Sun Belt.

To accommodate the influx of people and businesses, new housing
and offices have been constructed in record numbers. However,
overbuilding along the oceanfront has resulted in the erosion of many
east coast beaches. Reclamation projects currently are attempting to
solve the environmental problems Florida's population boom has
caused.

Florida's location also places it within easy reach of Caribbean and
Central American countries. Miami is considered the unofficial capital
of the Caribbean Islands and has become the destination of the poor,
exiled, and disenfranchised people of that area. The arrival of these
newcomers has put a heavy strain on the resources of both city and
state. Ironically, although Miami has absorbed the poor of many countries, it has also become a resort and shopping center for wealthy
Central and South Americans.

Although tourism and urban growth sometimes make destructive
demands upon natural resources, Florida's greatest resource—its climate—can never be depleted. And with its subtropical weather, resort
areas, and retirement communities, Florida provides a melding of rich
and poor, native resident and newcomer, natural beauty and modern
construction in this most northern of the southern states.

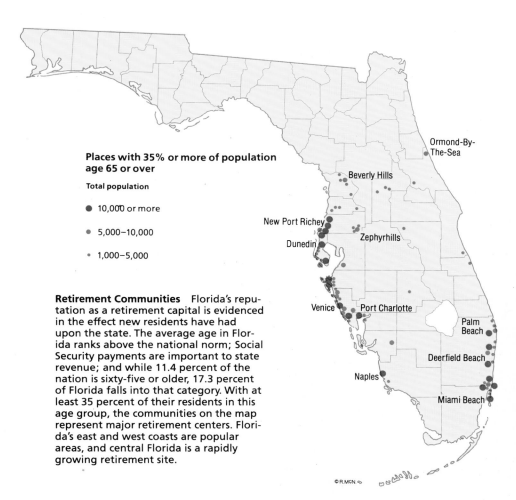

**Places with 35% or more of population
age 65 or over**

Total population

● 10,000 or more

● 5,000–10,000

· 1,000–5,000

Retirement Communities Florida's reputation as a retirement capital is evidenced
in the effect new residents have had
upon the state. The average age in Florida ranks above the national norm; Social
Security payments are important to state
revenue; and while 11.4 percent of the
nation is sixty-five or older, 17.3 percent
of Florida falls into that category. With at
least 35 percent of their residents in this
age group, the communities on the map
represent major retirement centers. Florida's east and west coasts are popular
areas, and central Florida is a rapidly
growing retirement site.

Land Use Much of the beauty and productivity of Florida's land is held in precar-
ious ecological balance. Although average temperature is high, sudden winter cold
spells can ruin citrus crops. Annual rainfall is also high, but variations can be harm-
ful to crops. Finally, most of Florida is no more than a hundred feet above sea level,
meaning many areas are subject to flooding and erosion.

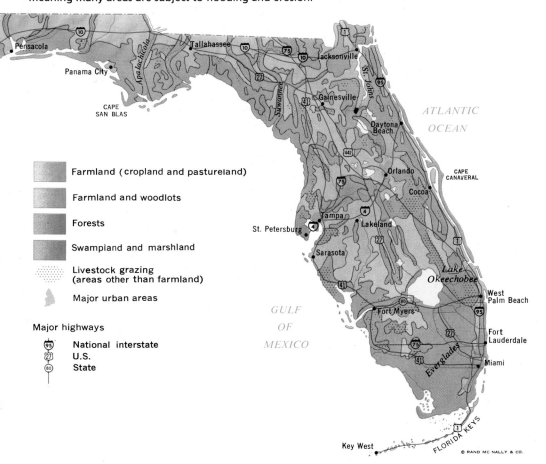

Farmland (cropland and pastureland)

Farmland and woodlots

Forests

Swampland and marshland

Livestock grazing
(areas other than farmland)

Major urban areas

Major highways

National interstate

U.S.

State

Home of the huge Kennedy Space Center, Cape Canaveral is
again in the limelight as a launch site for the Space Shuttle
program. Long important to the nation's science and
technology, the center also ensures the growth of Florida's
economy. High-technology industries are of major
importance in today's changing world, and in seeking an
ideal location for their businesses, these industries look at
both quality of life and local access to personnel. With the
benefits of its climate and the solid technological base
provided by the space center, Florida is selected more and
more often for expanding high-tech activities. Shown here is
the launch of the Space Shuttle *Challenger.*

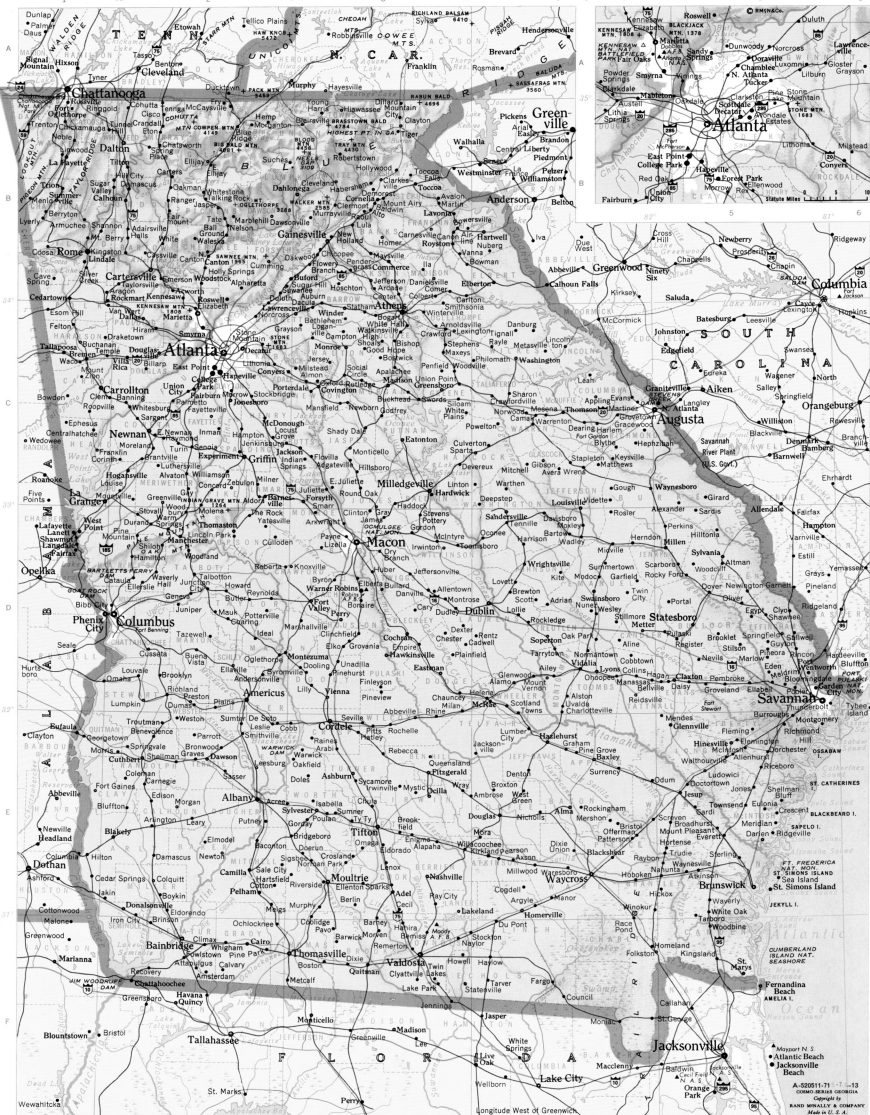

Cities and Towns

Adel 5,592 E3
Albany 74,550 E2
Americus 16,120 D2
Athens 42,549 C3
Atlanta 425,022 C2
Augusta 47,532 C5
Bainbridge 10,553 F2
Blakely 5,880 E2
Brunswick 17,605 E5
Buford 6,578 B2
Cairo 8,777 F2
Calhoun 5,563 B2
Camilla 5,414 E2
Carrollton 14,078 C1
Cartersville 9,247 B2
Cedartown 8,619 B1
Cochran 5,121 D3
College Park 24,632 C2
Columbus 169,441 D2
Cordele 11,184 E3
Covington 10,586 C3
Dalton 20,939 B2
Dawson 5,699 E2
Decatur 18,404 C2
Douglas 10,980 E4
Douglasville 7,641 C2
Dublin 16,083 D4
Eastman 5,330 D3
East Point 37,486 C2
Elberton 5,686 B4
Fitzgerald 10,187 E3
Forest Park 18,782 h8
Fort Oglethorpe 5,443 B1
Fort Valley 9,000 D3
Gainesville 15,280 B3
Griffin 20,728 C2
Hinesville 11,309 E5
Kennesaw 5,095 B2
La Fayette 6,517 B1
La Grange 24,204 C1
Lawrenceville 8,928 C3
Mableton 20,200 h7
Macon 116,896 D3
Marietta 30,829 C2
Martinez 16,472 C4
Milledgeville 12,176 C3
Monroe 8,854 C3
Moultrie 15,708 E3
Newnan 11,449 C2
North Atlanta 22,800 h8
Perry 9,453 D3
Quitman 5,188 F3
Rome 29,654 B1
Roswell 23,337 B2
St. Simons Island 6,566 E5
Sandersville 6,137 D4
Sandy Springs 20,300 h8
Savannah 141,390 D5
Smyrna 20,312 C2
Statesboro 14,866 D5
Stone Mountain 4,867 C2
Swainsboro 7,602 D4
Sylvester 5,860 E3
Thomaston 9,682 D2
Thomasville 18,463 F3
Thomson 7,001 C4
Tifton 13,749 E3
Toccoa 9,104 B3
Tucker 18,200 h8
Valdosta 37,596 F3
Vidalia 10,393 D4
Warner Robins 39,893 D3
Waycross 19,371 E4
Waynesboro 5,760 C4

Statute Miles 5 0 5 10 20 30 40
Kilometers 5 0 5 15 30 45 55

Lambert Conformal Conic Projection
SCALE 1:1,962,000   1 Inch = 31 Statute Miles

A-520511-71—7—13
COSMO SERIES GEORGIA
Copyright by
RAND McNALLY & COMPANY
Made in U.S.A.

Georgia

POPULATION 6,295,200.
Rank: 11.*Density:* 108 people/mi²
(42 people/km²).*Urban:*
62.4%.*Rural:* 37.6%.
INCOME/CAPITA $11,515.
Rank: 34.
ENTERED UNION Jan. 2, 1788,
4th state.

CAPITAL Atlanta, 451,200.
LARGEST CITY Atlanta.
LAND AREA 58,060 mi²
(150,375 km²).
Rank: 21.*Water area:* 854 mi²
(2,212 km²).
DIMENSIONS N–S 315 miles,
E–W 250 miles.

ELEVATIONS *Highest:* Brasstown
Bald, 4,784 ft (1,458 m).*Lowest:*
Atlantic Ocean shoreline, sea
level.
CLIMATE Humid with hot
summers, mild winters. Heavy
rainfall in northeast.

Georgia has long been one of the economic and cultural leaders of the South. In the past, transportation routes and a prosperous agriculture contributed to Georgia's influence. Today, Atlanta, Georgia's largest city, is the hub of regional transportation networks, a center for business, and often called the Capital of the New South. In its successful transition from the agriculture of the Old South to the diversified economy of the New South, Georgia has become the focus of national as well as regional attention.

Yet in many ways, Georgia is still a state in transition. While Atlanta is a cosmopolitan area, drawing people and businesses from across the country, income in some nearby rural regions falls far below the national average. Many of these areas focus primarily on rural concerns, operating outside the state's current trend toward economic diversification. Yet the income disparities between city and rural dwellers, along with their regional differences, are slowly being recognized and overcome.

While Georgia's agriculture remains important, that agriculture has changed dramatically in the last hundred years. Cotton, formerly king here as in many southern states, now shares its throne with other important crops. Farming is diversified and mechanized, and in many areas, farms are run as businesses or corporations. As a result, more and more rural families have been leaving the land to move to the cities. Most still work in farm- or forest-related industries, such as poultry processing, lumber milling, and turning cotton into textiles and carpeting. These and other activities make industry rather than agriculture the prime source of revenue for the state. Economic and social changes resulting from the growth and spread of manufacturing are helping to unite regions that have been divided since the state's early history, and Georgia is also seeking ways to diminish divisions between whites and blacks in its society.

Industrial growth and regional and social integration will most likely continue as Georgia's transition from Old South to New South becomes complete. In working toward its economic and cultural goals, the state may well serve as a model for its neighbors, strengthening its traditional position as a leader of the South.

Atlanta symbolizes the successful city of the New South. In *Places Rated Almanac*, a publication ranking United States metropolitan areas, Atlanta scored the highest for general quality of life, which included factors such as education, housing, and recreation.

Land Use Although not the major activity it once was, agriculture is still important in Georgia. Soil erosion has long been a problem, however; and today, it is controlled by contour plowing, terracing, reforestation, and other conservation practices. In addition to reducing soil runoff, reforestation contributes to the growth of Georgia's forest-products industry.

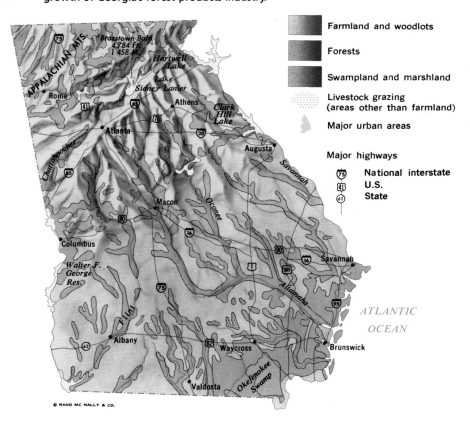

Farmland and woodlots

Forests

Swampland and marshland

Livestock grazing
(areas other than farmland)

Major urban areas

Major highways

National interstate
U.S.
State

© RAND MC NALLY & CO.

ATLANTIC
OCEAN

Employment Trends Georgia's changing economy is evidenced by shifts in employment, and these reflect the transition from the agriculture of the Old South to the industry of the New South occurring throughout the Southeast. Once the state's major employer, agriculture has been overshadowed by manufacturing, and agricultural employment has dropped off dramatically. This is partially due to increased mechanization, but changing economic emphasis is the main cause. Manufacturing in the state is becoming more and more diversified, and future stability is ensured by the greater-than-average growth of high-technology industries. And as manufacturing increases in importance, other areas of the economy are affected. Wholesale and retail trade and service industries, for example, show the effects of growth in the manufacturing sector.

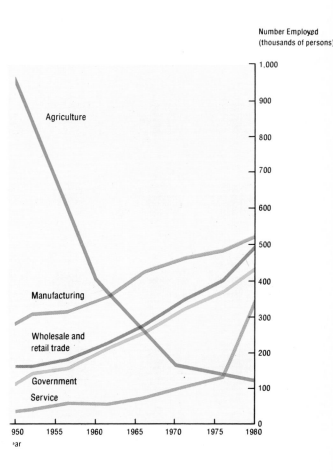

Number Employed
(thousands of persons)

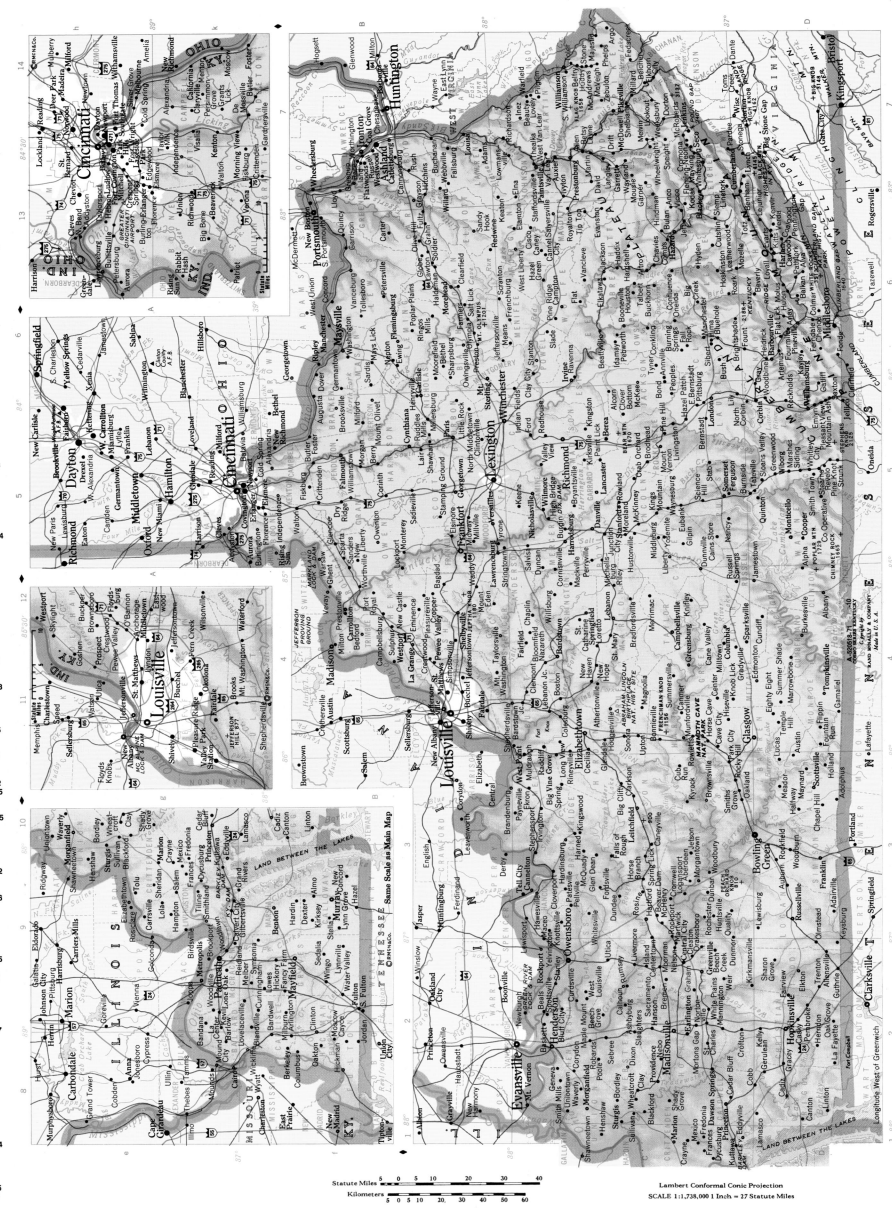

Cities and Towns

Alexandria 4,735 **B5**
Ashland 27,064 **B7**
Barbourville 3,333 **D6**
Bardstown 6,155 **C4**
Berea 8,226 **C5**
Bowling Green 40,450 **D3**
Campbellsville 8,715 **C4**
Carrollton 3,967 **B4**
Cave City 2,098 **C4**
Central City 5,214 **C2**
Corbin 8,075 **D5**
Covington 49,563 **A5**
Cynthiana 5,881 **B5**
Danville 12,942 **C5**
Edgewood 7,230 **h13**
Elizabethtown 15,380 **C4**
Elsmere 7,203 **B5**
Erlanger 14,433 **A5**
Fairdale 7,315 **B4**
Fern Creek 16,866 **g11**
Flatwoods 8,354 **B7**
Florence 15,586 **A5**
Fort Mitchell 7,297 **h13**
Fort Thomas 16,012 **h14**
Frankfort 25,973 **B5**
Franklin 7,738 **D3**
Georgetown 10,972 **B5**
Glasgow 12,958 **C4**
Greenville 4,631 **C2**
Harrodsburg 7,265 **C5**
Hazard 5,371 **C6**
Henderson 24,834 **C2**
Hopkinsville 27,318 **D2**
Independence 7,998 **B5**
Jeffersontown 15,795 **B4**
Lawrenceburg 5,167 **B5**
Lebanon 6,590 **C4**
Leitchfield 4,533 **C3**
Lexington 204,165 **B5**
London 4,002 **C5**
Louisville 298,840 **B4**
Madisonville 16,979 **C2**
Mayfield 10,705 **f9**
Maysville 7,983 **B6**
Middlesboro 12,251 **D6**
Monticello 5,677 **D5**
Morehead 7,789 **B6**
Mount Sterling 5,820 **B6**
Murray 14,248 **f9**
Newport 21,587 **A5**
Nicholasville 10,319 **C5**
Okolona 20,039 **g11**
Owensboro 54,450 **C2**
Paducah 29,315 **e9**
Paris 7,935 **B5**
Pikeville 4,756 **C7**
Pleasure Ridge Park 27,332 **g11**
Prestonsburg 4,011 **C7**
Providence 4,434 **C2**
Radcliff 14,519 **C4**
Richmond 21,705 **C5**
Russellville 7,520 **D3**
St. Matthews 13,519 **B4**
Scottsville 4,278 **D3**
Shelbyville 5,329 **B4**
Shepherdsville 4,454 **C4**
Shively 16,819 **B4**
Somerset 10,649 **C5**
Tompkinsville 4,366 **D4**
Valley Station 20,000 **g11**
Versailles 6,427 **B5**
Westwood 5,973 **B7**
Williamsburg 5,560 **D5**
Winchester 15,216 **C5**

Statute Miles
Kilometers

Lambert Conformal Conic Projection
SCALE 1:1,738,000 1 Inch = 27 Statute Miles

Kentucky

POPULATION   3,771,500.
Rank: 23.*Density:* 95 people/mi²
(37 people/km²).*Urban:*
50.9%.*Rural:* 49.1%.
INCOME/CAPITA $10,401.
Rank: 41.
ENTERED UNION   June 1, 1792,
15th state.

CAPITAL   Frankfort, 26,900.
LARGEST CITY   Louisville, 285,200.
LAND AREA   39,674 mi²
(102,755 km²).
Rank: 37.*Water area:* 740 mi²
(1,917 km²).
DIMENSIONS   N–S 175 miles,
E–W 350 miles.

ELEVATIONS   *Highest:* Black
Mountain, 4,145 ft
(1,263 m).*Lowest:* Along
Mississippi River, 257 ft (78 m).
CLIMATE   Hot summers, short
winters with some snow;
moderate rainfall.

For stirring the romantic imagination, Kentucky has few rivals. The state's name conjures images of Daniel Boone, Abraham Lincoln, and Jefferson Davis; coal miners, moonshiners, and mountaineers; and white-suited colonels, bourbon whiskey, and the Kentucky Derby. Behind each image and legend lies a bit of truth about Kentucky and the historical diversity of its culture and landscape.

The legends of famous pioneers and statesmen reflect Kentucky's long history as a boundary state. It first marked the line between the eastern seaboard and America's great western frontier. During the Civil War, the state straddled the boundary between North and South, torn in the struggle that bitterly divided the nation, attempting to maintain neutrality.

Generations of coal miners have worked Kentucky's Appalachian Highlands and the coalfields east of the Tennessee River, two of the leading coal-producing regions of the country. Contrasts of wealth and poverty have plagued these regions for decades, and more recently, those who favor continued coal development have clashed with those seeking to save the land from the devastating effects of strip-mining.

The central Bluegrass basin brings to mind gentlemen farmers and colonels with their fine bourbon and prize thoroughbred horses. Like the neighboring Pennyroyal area and the far western corner of the state, this region is one of Kentucky's prime livestock and agricultural producers. In eastern upland Kentucky, timber is an important part of the economy, and this area is justly proud of its wood products and furniture. In addition, manufacturing has created a landscape of cities and industrial sites, particularly along the Ohio River, that are well known for tobacco products, whiskey, and a variety of industrial goods.

Throughout history, the special character of each of Kentucky's regions has contributed much of its romantic image. But today, economic stability requires regional integration, and distinctions are lost in working for the good of the state as a whole. Yet no matter how modern Kentucky may become, the legends of the past will continue to influence the nation's image of this diverse land.

Within the Bluegrass region of north-central Kentucky lies the state's most productive agricultural land, with its peaceful scenes of grazing horses, gently rolling meadows, and tobacco fields.

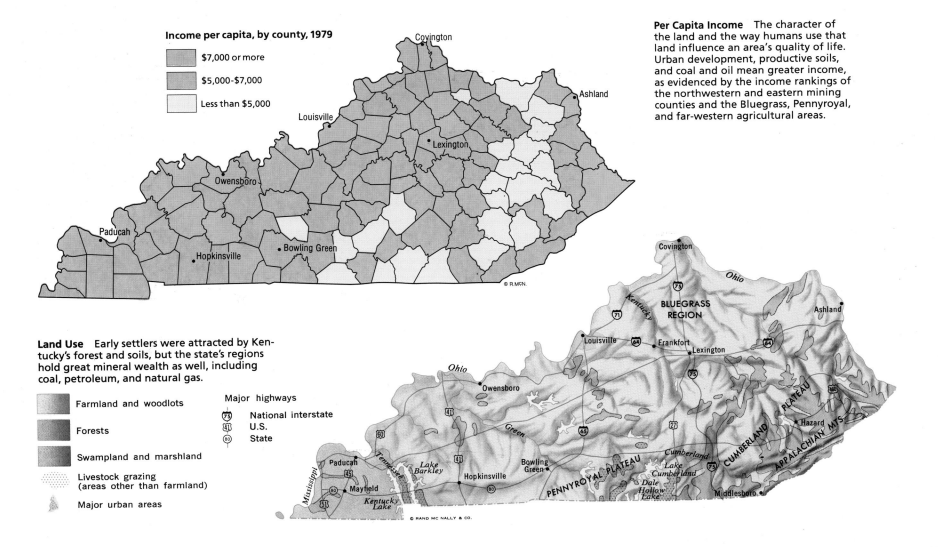

Income per capita, by county, 1979

- $7,000 or more
- $5,000–$7,000
- Less than $5,000

Per Capita Income   The character of the land and the way humans use that land influence an area's quality of life. Urban development, productive soils, and coal and oil mean greater income, as evidenced by the income rankings of the northwestern and eastern mining counties and the Bluegrass, Pennyroyal, and far-western agricultural areas.

Land Use   Early settlers were attracted by Kentucky's forest and soils, but the state's regions hold great mineral wealth as well, including coal, petroleum, and natural gas.

- Farmland and woodlots
- Forests
- Swampland and marshland
- Livestock grazing (areas other than farmland)
- Major urban areas

Major highways
- 75 National interstate
- 41 U.S.
- 80 State

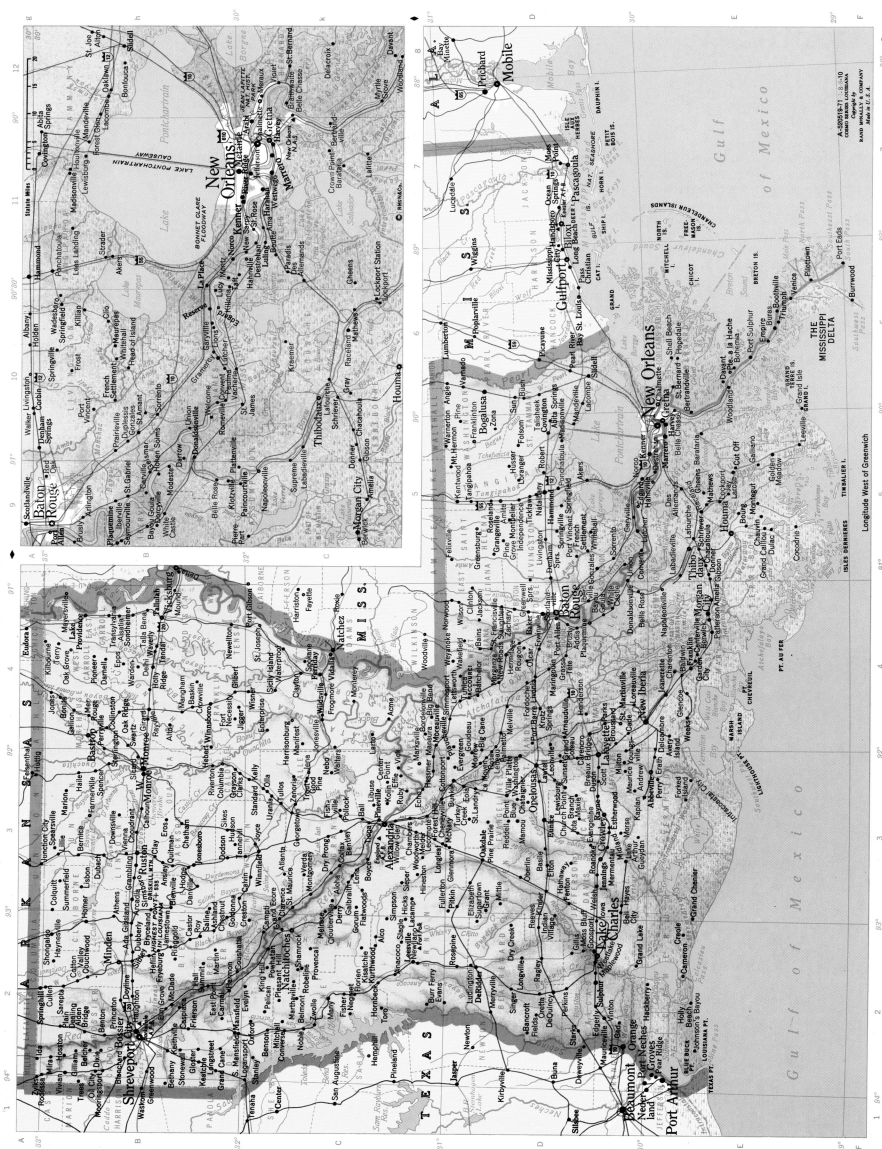

Cities and Towns

Abbeville 12,391 **E3**
Alexandria 51,565 **C3**
Arabi 10,248 **k11**
Baker 12,865 **D4**
Bastrop 15,527 **B4**
Baton Rouge 219,419 **D4**
Bogalusa 16,976 **D6**
Bossier City 50,817 **B2**
Breaux Bridge 5,922 **D4**
Bunkie 5,364 **D4**
Chalmette 33,847 **E6**
Covington 7,892 **D5**
Crowley 16,036 **D3**
Denham Springs 8,563 **D5**
De Ridder 11,057 **D2**
Donaldsonville 7,901 **D4**
Eunice 12,479 **D3**
Franklin 9,584 **E4**
Galliano 5,159 **E5**
Gonzales 7,287 **D5**
Grambling 4,226 **B3**
Gretna 20,615 **E5**
Hammond 15,043 **D5**
Harahan 11,384 **k11**
Harvey 15,000 **E5**
Houma 32,602 **E5**
Jeanerette 6,511 **E4**
Jefferson 15,550 **k11**
Jena 4,375 **C3**
Jennings 12,401 **D3**
Jonesboro 5,061 **B3**
Kaplan 5,016 **D3**
Kenner 66,382 **E5**
Lacombe 5,146 **D6**
Lafayette 81,961 **D3**
Lake Charles 75,226 **D2**
Lake Providence 6,361 **B4**
La Place 16,112 **h11**
Leesville 9,054 **C2**
Mandeville 6,076 **D5**
Mansfield 6,485 **B2**
Marrero 36,548 **E5**
Metairie 164,160 **k11**
Minden 15,084 **B2**
Monroe 57,597 **B3**
Morgan City 16,114 **E4**
Moss Bluff 7,004 **D2**
Natchitoches 16,664 **C2**
New Iberia 32,766 **D4**
New Orleans 557,927 **E5**
Oakdale 7,155 **D3**
Opelousas 18,903 **D3**
Pineville 12,034 **C3**
Plaquemine 7,521 **D4**
Raceland 6,302 **E5**
Rayne 9,066 **D3**
Reserve 7,288 **h10**
River Ridge 17,146 **k11**
Ruston 20,585 **B3**
St. Martinville 7,965 **D4**
Scotlandville 15,113 **D4**
Shreveport 205,820 **B2**
Slidell 26,718 **D6**
Springhill 6,516 **A2**
Sulphur 19,709 **D2**
Tallulah 11,634 **B4**
Thibodaux 15,810 **E5**
Vidalia 5,936 **C4**
Ville Platte 9,201 **D3**
West Monroe 14,993 **B3**
Westwego 12,663 **k11**
Winnfield 7,311 **C3**
Winnsboro 5,921 **B4**
Zachary 7,297 **D4**

Statute Miles
Kilometers

Lambert Conformal Conic Projection
SCALE 1:2,083,000   1 Inch = 33 Statute Miles

Louisiana

POPULATION 4,517,800.
Rank: 20.*Density:* 101 people/mi²
(39 people/km²).*Urban:*
68.6%.*Rural:* 31.4%.
INCOME/CAPITA $9,999.
Rank: 44.
ENTERED UNION April 30, 1812,
18th state.

CAPITAL Baton Rouge, 245,200.
LARGEST CITY New Orleans,
557,700.
LAND AREA 44,520 mi²
(115,306 km²).
Rank: 33.*Water area:* 3,230 mi²
(8,366 km²).
DIMENSIONS N–S 275 miles,
E–W 300 miles.

ELEVATIONS *Highest:* Driskill
Mountain, 535 ft (163 m).*Lowest:*
New Orleans, 5 ft (2 m) below
sea level.
CLIMATE Humid with long, hot
summers; short, mild winters.
Moderately heavy rainfall.

M uch of Louisiana's history and culture has been shaped by the Mississippi River and the state's Spanish and French heritage. Even its legal system is based on French civil law rather than English common law, found in all other states. New Orleans, near the head of the river delta, is one of America's great ports, serving as the main entryway into the central part of the country.

But Louisiana's prime location did not always guarantee prosperity. At one time, the state was greatly dependent upon agriculture, and not until World War II did Louisiana experience real growth. The wartime demand for port facilities set Louisiana on its present course of rapid diversification and expansion, and soon manufacturing surpassed agriculture in importance. The discovery of land-based oil and gas spurred further development in establishing chemical industries. And when petroleum reserves were found in the Gulf of Mexico, southern Louisiana became important for offshore drilling.

Although agriculture no longer dominates Louisiana's economy, it is still important. The state's near-tropical climate and rich delta soil are ideal for crops such as soybeans, rice, cotton, and sugarcane. The Mississippi River is both creator and destroyer, however, since the floods that renew the delta soil also devastate nearby cities and towns. Much of the state lies close to sea level, and the banks of the river continue to build up because of flooding. As a result, drainage in crop fields is a chronic problem for farmers.

The river has also fragmented the geography and population of the state. The southern area is dominated by New Orleans, whose French Quarter is a charming reminder of the early French and Spanish presence. Coastal waterways and winding channels of the Mississippi Delta cut the southern region into enclaves, isolating one group of people from another. Partially due to this isolation, the Cajuns, who resettled from Nova Scotia in the eighteenth century, have preserved their culture and French dialect for over two hundred years.

Like many southern states, Louisiana has experienced rapid economic development in the past decades. And in maintaining its unique blend of old and new, the state still looks to the Mississippi River and a colorful and varied past.

Bird Migration Over half the known North American bird species have been recorded in Louisiana, and one reason is the Mississippi Flyway that crosses the state. This is the longest and most heavily traveled of the four major American flyways. Each year millions of migrating birds pass through Louisiana, some stopping only for a short time, others remaining for a season before moving on.

Migration routes

Forest
Swamp or marsh
Wildlife refuge

Bird Habitats Louisiana is a natural bird aviary, with forests, swamps, rivers, and plains providing homes for many types of birds. But the wetlands especially play a major role. In addition to migrating birds, over ninety species live in the marshes year-round. Conservation activities ensure the continued presence of wildlife.

Land Use The Mississippi River sets Louisiana apart from many of its neighbors on the Coastal Plain of the Gulf of Mexico. The river deposits valuable alluvial soil along its banks and delta channels but always threatens the state with destructive flooding. The Mississippi Delta contains the most fertile land in the state due to riverine deposition, but when the Mississippi tops its banks, most of the region faces flooding that can result in great loss of life and property.

Farmland (cropland and pastureland)

Farmland and woodlots

Forests

Swampland and marshland

Livestock grazing (areas other than farmland)

Major urban areas

Major highways

National interstate

U.S.

Canal

Louisiana's heritage is reflected in the architecture of the French Quarter in New Orleans. Originally settled by the French, the Louisiana area was under Spanish rule when fires swept through New Orleans in the late 1700's. The Spanish style of architecture used in rebuilding can be seen today in the intricate iron grillwork gracing the balconies of many buildings.

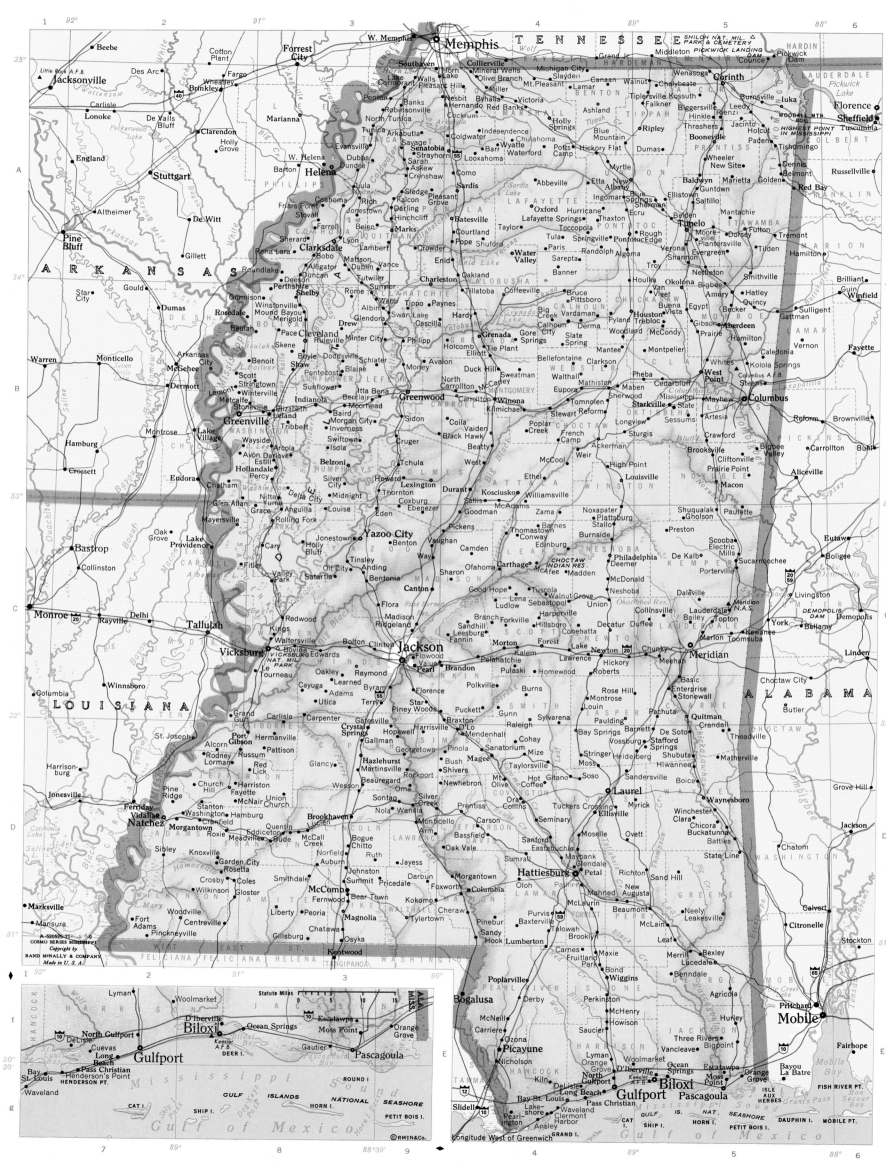

COSMO SERIES MISSISSIPPI
Copyright by
RAND McNALLY & COMPANY
Made in U.S.A.

A-520525-21 · · 5-5-bg

Statute Miles 5 0 5 10 20 30 40
Kilometers 5 0 5 15 25 35 45 55

Lambert Conformal Conic Projection
SCALE 1:1,837,000 1 Inch = 29 Statute Miles

©RMcN&Co.

Mississippi

POPULATION 2,676,200.
Rank: 31.*Density:* 57 people/mi²
(22 people/km²).*Urban:*
47.3%.*Rural:* 52.7%.
INCOME/CAPITA $8,599.
Rank: 50.
ENTERED UNION Dec. 10, 1817,
20th state.

CAPITAL Jackson, 212,900.
LARGEST CITY Jackson.
LAND AREA 47,234 mi²
(122,335 km²).
Rank: 31.*Water area:* 457 mi²
(1,184 km²).
DIMENSIONS N–S 340 miles,
E–W 180 miles.

ELEVATIONS *Highest:* Woodall
Mountain, 806 ft (246 m).*Lowest:*
Gulf of Mexico shoreline, sea
level.
CLIMATE Long, hot, humid
summers with thundershowers;
short, mild winters.

Nothing in Mississippi's terrain as it changes from flatlands to gently rolling hills betrays the extremes of its economic, educational, and political systems. Yet the state must balance these extremes to create new wealth and stability for the future.

Mississippi's economy is at a disadvantage partly because many of its natural resources are best suited for agriculture in an industrial nation and its population is still mainly rural in a highly urbanized country. To achieve progress, Mississippi must move into the prevailing industrial-urban national economy. The state has already taken some steps in that direction, as evidenced by the growth of industry in a number of cities. Such efforts have been supported by investors and companies in other southern and northern states, who are finding Mississippi attractive as a business site.

Despite its economic problems, Mississippi has in a sense contributed to national wealth, particularly in the field of American literature. Such writers as Tennessee Williams, Eudora Welty, and William Faulkner have drawn from their Mississippi experiences for much of their rich material. And the state's educational system has been involved in a series of reforms aimed at improved standards and increased enrollment.

Economic and cultural differences are at times heightened by Mississippi's political conflicts. Even before the Civil War, and in the years following, the population was divided politically, and some of these differences have remained unresolved. Recently, the state has begun to move toward ensuring greater political equality among the wealthier segment of society, the white farmers working small family farms inland from the Mississippi Delta, and the predominantly rural black population.

In the future, Mississippi is sure to reap some of the benefits of the South's rapid growth over the past decades. Businesses are turning more and more to the southern states, lured by liberal tax laws and low-cost labor. The people of Mississippi can take pride in their efforts to balance the extremes of their economic, social, and political lives and can look forward to a future of growth and prosperity.

Tourism Since World War II, tourism has been at a significant level in Mississippi, but over the past fifteen years it has developed into a dynamic state business. Part of this increase can be attributed to the extension and improvement of the state's highway system. Some of the most rapid growth has occurred in the Natchez, Vicksburg, and Gulf Coast areas. Mississippi's economy has been greatly strengthened by the revenue brought through tourism.

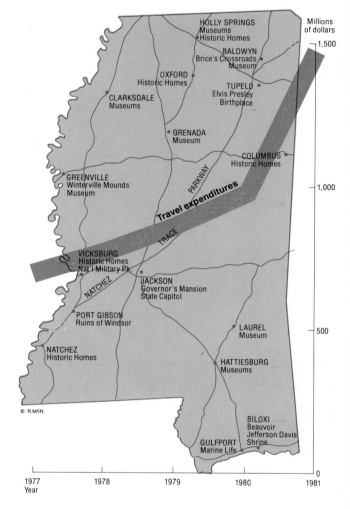

Land Use Mississippi provides an excellent environment for agriculture and forestry. Water is, perhaps, too plentiful, with floods posing more of a threat than droughts. More importantly, heavy rains contribute to a serious soil-erosion problem. Not only is much soil lost to sheet erosion and gullying on hilly upland slopes, but this eroded material, sometimes less fertile, is then deposited on top of richer alluvial soils in river valleys. Nevertheless, great progress has been made in protecting vulnerable slopes, river valleys, and watersheds.

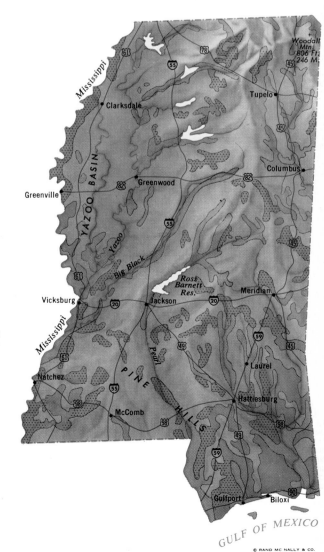

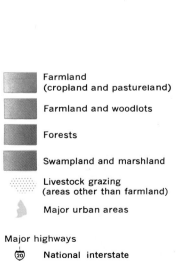

While economies reflect the trend of industrialization occurring throughout the South, many landmarks recall the region's pre-Civil War society. Mississippi plays a major role in preserving southern traditions, and Natchez is the site of graceful mansions that recreate the atmosphere of antebellum days. Careful maintenance of historic structures displays the state's attempt to balance modernization with its Old South heritage.

Farmland
(cropland and pastureland)

Farmland and woodlots

Forests

Swampland and marshland

Livestock grazing
(areas other than farmland)

Major urban areas

Major highways
  National interstate
  U.S.

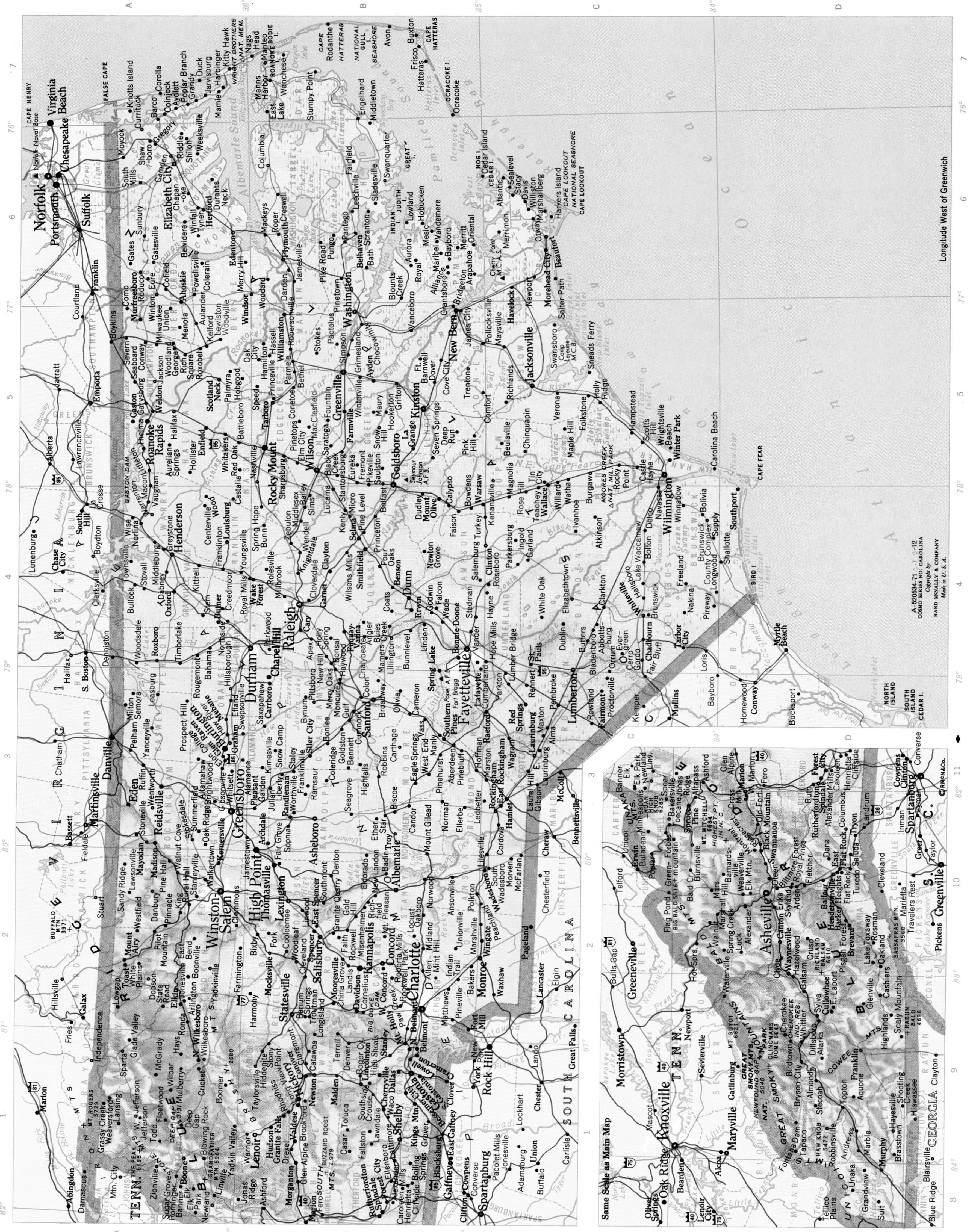

Cities and Towns

Albemarle 15,110 **B2**
Archdale 5,326 **B3**
Asheboro 15,252 **B3**
Asheville 53,583 **f10**
Boone 10,191 **A1**
Brevard 5,323 **f10**
Burlington 37,266 **A3**
Carrboro 7,336 **B3**
Chapel Hill 32,421 **B3**
Charlotte 314,447 **B2**
Clemmons 7,401 **A2**
Clinton 7,552 **C4**
Concord 16,942 **B2**
Dunn 8,962 **B4**
Durham 100,538 **B4**
Eden 15,672 **A3**
Edenton 5,357 **A6**
Elizabeth City 13,784 **A6**
Fayetteville 59,507 **B4**
Forest City 7,688 **B1**
Garner 10,073 **B4**
Gastonia 47,333 **B1**
Goldsboro 31,871 **B5**
Graham 8,674 **A3**
Greensboro 155,642 **A3**
Greenville 35,740 **B5**
Havelock 17,718 **C6**
Henderson 13,522 **A4**
Hendersonville 6,862 **f10**
Hickory 20,757 **B1**
High Point 63,808 **B2**
Jacksonville 18,237 **C5**
Kannapolis 34,564 **B2**
Kernersville 6,802 **A2**
Kings Mountain 9,080 **B1**
Kinston 25,234 **B5**
Laurinburg 11,480 **C3**
Lenoir 13,748 **B1**
Lexington 15,711 **B2**
Lincolnton 4,879 **B1**
Lumberton 18,241 **C3**
Monroe 12,639 **C2**
Mooresville 8,575 **B2**
Morehead City 4,359 **C6**
Morganton 13,763 **B1**
Mount Airy 6,862 **A2**
Mount Olive 4,876 **B4**
Nags Head 1,020 **B7**
New Bern 14,557 **B5**
Newton 7,624 **B1**
Oxford 7,603 **A4**
Plymouth 4,571 **B6**
Raleigh 150,255 **B4**
Reidsville 12,492 **A3**
Roanoke Rapids 14,702 **A5**
Rockingham 8,300 **C3**
Rocky Mount 41,283 **B5**
Roxboro 7,532 **A4**
Salisbury 22,677 **B2**
Sanford 14,773 **B3**
Selma 4,762 **B4**
Shelby 15,310 **B1**
Smithfield 7,288 **B4**
Southern Pines 8,620 **B3**
Statesville 18,622 **B2**
Swannanoa 5,586 **f10**
Tarboro 8,634 **B5**
Thomasville 14,144 **B2**
Washington 8,418 **B5**
Whiteville 5,565 **C4**
Williamston 6,159 **B5**
Wilmington 44,000 **C5**
Wilson 34,424 **B5**
Winston-Salem 131,885 **A2**

A-50058A-71
COSMO SERIES NO. CAROLINA
Copyright by
RAND McNALLY & COMPANY
Made in U.S.A.

Statute Miles
Kilometers

Same Scale as Main Map

Lambert Conformal Conic Projection
SCALE 1:1,950,000   1 Inch = 31 Statute Miles

North Carolina

POPULATION 6,463,600.
Rank: 10.*Density:* 132 people/mi²
(51 people/km²).*Urban:*
48.0%.*Rural:* 52.0%.
INCOME/CAPITA $11,061.
Rank: 37.
ENTERED UNION Nov. 21, 1789,
12th state.

CAPITAL Raleigh, 199,000.
LARGEST CITY Charlotte, 375,000.
LAND AREA 48,843 mi²
(126,503 km²).
Rank: 29.*Water area:* 3,826 mi²
(9,909 km²).
DIMENSIONS N–S 200 miles,
E–W 520 miles.

ELEVATIONS *Highest:* Mount
Mitchell, 6,684 ft
(2,037 m).*Lowest:* Atlantic Ocean
shoreline, sea level.
CLIMATE Hot summers, mild
winters in east. Cool summers,
cold winters, heavy rain in west.

In many ways, North Carolina has had to wait until the twentieth century to be fully discovered. Perhaps this is fitting, for the state contains ruins of the Lost Colony, the first English settlement in America, which met a mysterious end in the 1580's.

From early colonial days, settlement of the state was slow. Its rich Piedmont country of low, rolling hills is sandwiched between lowlands to the east, made inaccessible by the treacherous Atlantic coast, and mountains to the west. Pioneers seeking more accessible land to farm bypassed the region on their way south and west. Even when immigrants managed to navigate the coastline, they found little more than marshes and swamp—many discouraged travelers even refused to land. In addition, since the Appalachian Mountains made North Carolina a poor route to America's interior, the state did not have the chance to attract pioneers who otherwise would have been traveling through it. Nor could North Carolina take advantage of the railroad boom in the late nineteenth century. When tracks might have been laid across the Piedmont, linking northern and southern states, North Carolina was too financially drained and politically divided from the Civil War to finance construction.

Today, after a hundred years of development, a network of highways and railroads has penetrated North Carolina's heartland, helping the state realize its economic potential. Its resources of coal, water, minerals, forests, and industrial products make North Carolina one of the most powerful industrial states in the South.

However, in spite of its recovery and its growing strength, North Carolina faces problems brought on by changes outside its borders. Its textile industry is threatened by foreign competition, and its tobacco crop may be hard hit by increasing antismoking campaigns.

Even so, as a forward-looking state, North Carolina has already begun to grapple with these realities. Its "research triangle," anchored by major universities in Durham, Raleigh, and Chapel Hill, is providing the technological resources to solve these and other problems. Slow to be explored and settled, North Carolina is discovering itself and its prospects for a still brighter future.

While North Carolina's Outer Banks provide the mainland with a natural protection from ocean tempests, the islands themselves are left subject to severe wind and wave erosion. The shifting, unstable nature of the sandy islands makes them largely unsuitable for development, and two national seashores have been established to protect both the land and the people. There are a number of small fishing villages along the chain of islands, but as can be seen here, wave erosion continues to be a problem for residents.

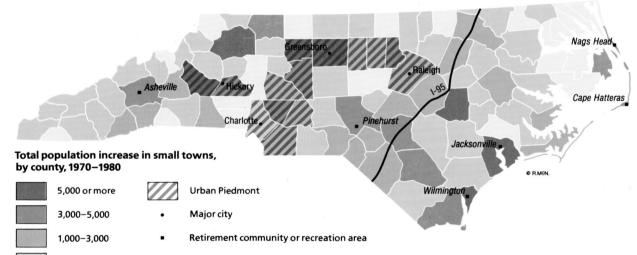

Total population increase in small towns, by county, 1970–1980

■ 5,000 or more	▨ Urban Piedmont
■ 3,000–5,000	• Major city
▨ 1,000–3,000	▪ Retirement community or recreation area
▨ 1–1,000	
□ Decrease	

(small town = population under 5,000 as of 1970)

Small-Town Growth Recent developments in North Carolina have led to population growth in small towns. Increased industrialization of the cities in North Carolina's central Piedmont has expanded the population of the region's small towns, many of which serve as bedroom communities for the larger cities. Since the completion of I-95 through the state, manufacturing employment along its corridor has grown, and this, too, has led to an increase. Also furthering small-town growth has been the increase in recreation and retirement areas along the coast and in the uplands.

Land Use Because of treacherous waters and tidewater swamps, North Carolina's important cities and farmland are located far from the Atlantic and are connected to the North and South by overland routes. These inland paths are preferred to water routes, since they link North Carolina's rich Piedmont region more directly with its extension in other states.

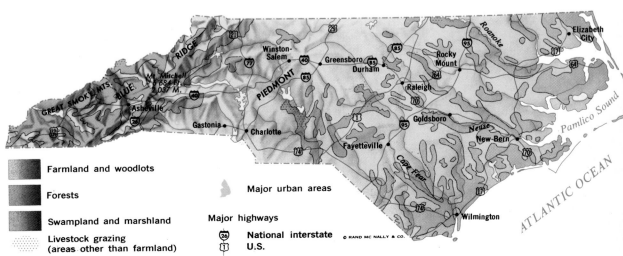

▨ Farmland and woodlots	
▨ Forests	▲ Major urban areas
▨ Swampland and marshland	Major highways
▨ Livestock grazing (areas other than farmland)	ⓜ National interstate ⓤ U.S.

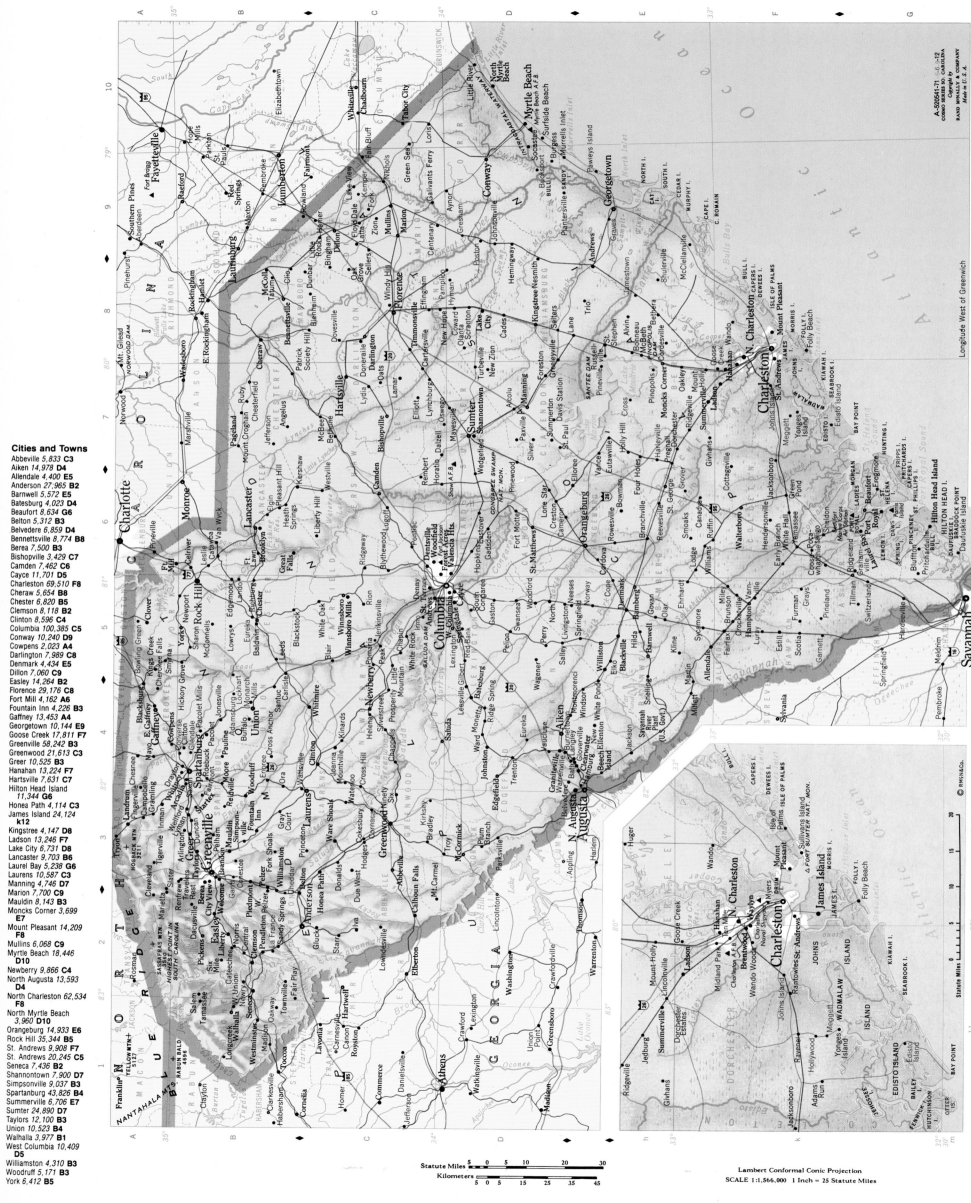

Cities and Towns

Abbeville 5,833 **C3**
Aiken 14,978 **D4**
Allendale 4,400 **E5**
Anderson 27,965 **B2**
Barnwell 5,572 **E5**
Batesburg 4,023 **D4**
Beaufort 8,634 **G6**
Belton 5,312 **B3**
Belvedere 6,859 **D4**
Bennettsville 8,774 **B8**
Berea 7,500 **B3**
Bishopville 3,429 **C7**
Camden 7,462 **C6**
Cayce 11,701 **D5**
Charleston 69,510 **F8**
Cheraw 5,654 **B8**
Chester 6,820 **B5**
Clemson 8,118 **B2**
Clinton 8,596 **C4**
Columbia 100,385 **C5**
Conway 10,240 **D9**
Cowpens 2,023 **A4**
Darlington 7,989 **C8**
Denmark 4,434 **E5**
Dillon 7,060 **C9**
Easley 14,264 **B2**
Florence 29,176 **C8**
Fort Mill 4,162 **A6**
Fountain Inn 4,226 **B3**
Gaffney 13,453 **A4**
Georgetown 10,144 **E9**
Goose Creek 17,811 **F7**
Greenville 58,242 **B3**
Greenwood 21,613 **C3**
Greer 10,525 **B3**
Hanahan 13,224 **F7**
Hartsville 7,631 **C7**
Hilton Head Island
   11,344 **G6**
Honea Path 4,114 **C3**
James Island 24,124
   k12
Kingstree 4,147 **D8**
Ladson 13,246 **F7**
Lake City 6,731 **D8**
Lancaster 9,703 **B6**
Laurel Bay 5,238 **G6**
Laurens 10,587 **C3**
Manning 4,746 **D7**
Marion 7,700 **C9**
Mauldin 8,143 **B3**
Moncks Corner 3,699
   E7
Mount Pleasant 14,209
   F8
Mullins 6,068 **C9**
Myrtle Beach 18,446
   D10
Newberry 9,866 **C4**
North Augusta 13,593
   D4
North Charleston 62,534
   F8
North Myrtle Beach
   3,960 **D10**
Orangeburg 14,933 **E6**
Rock Hill 35,344 **B5**
St. Andrews 9,908 **F7**
St. Andrews 20,245 **C5**
Seneca 7,436 **B2**
Shannontown 7,900 **D7**
Simpsonville 9,037 **B3**
Spartanburg 43,826 **B4**
Summerville 6,706 **E7**
Sumter 24,890 **D7**
Taylors 12,100 **B3**
Union 10,523 **B4**
Walhalla 3,977 **B1**
West Columbia 10,409
   D5
Williamston 4,310 **B3**
Woodruff 5,171 **B3**
York 6,412 **B5**

Statute Miles
Kilometers

Lambert Conformal Conic Projection
SCALE 1:1,566,000   1 Inch = 25 Statute Miles

South Carolina

POPULATION 3,458,400.
Rank: 24.*Density:* 114 people/mi²
(44 people/km²).*Urban:*
54.1%.*Rural:* 45.9%.
INCOME/CAPITA $10,042.
Rank: 43.
ENTERED UNION May 23, 1788,
8th state.

CAPITAL Columbia, 95,300.
LARGEST CITY Columbia.
LAND AREA 30,207 mi²
(78,236 km²).
Rank: 40.*Water area:* 909 mi²
(2,354 km²).
DIMENSIONS N–S 215 miles,
E–W 285 miles.

ELEVATIONS *Highest:* Sassafras
Mountain, 3,560 ft
(1,085 m).*Lowest:* Atlantic Ocean
shoreline, sea level.
CLIMATE Humid with long, hot
summers; short, mild winters.

More than some southeastern states, South Carolina reflects the tradition of the Old South. This is expressed in the particularly southern atmosphere found in the countryside and towns, with their beautiful flower gardens and graceful architecture, and in the customs, manners, and everyday life of South Carolina's people. Yet at the same time, the state is one of the best developed and most economically varied southern states, similar to many industrialized regions in the North. Perhaps its economic success has enabled South Carolina to retain the finer points of its cultural traditions.

Mention South Carolina and most people are likely to imagine cotton fields and a slow, leisurely pace of life. But time has brought many changes, and that image is no longer representative of the state as a whole. Tobacco, soybeans, cotton, and peaches remain strong products in South Carolina, but today there are fewer farms and less land under cultivation than a few decades ago. In fact, the state has expanded into nearly every class of manufactured goods from paper to chemicals to primary metals, with the textile industry the dominant business. In addition, since World War II, naval, marine, army, and air-force installations have aided the state's development.

South Carolina has also made progress in creating a more racially and regionally balanced culture. The state is fortunate that its division into distinct regions—defined by the Atlantic Coastal Plain, Piedmont Plateau, and Blue Ridge Mountains—has not created the factionalism experienced in some neighboring states. However, South Carolina's traditional conservatism is dictating a slow, careful pace toward greater social integration and welfare.

Unlike states that have broken with the past to move rapidly into present trends, South Carolina today continues to blend the old and the new. It has always been proud of its traditions and maintains a sense of history that is likely to influence the state's development in the coming decades.

Founded in 1670, Charleston is South Carolina's oldest and one of the country's most historic cities. Its unique blend of Old and New South reflects the state's pride in the past and its success in the present. Many carefully preserved buildings date to pre-Civil War days, and Charleston's architecture, streets, and parks tell of the state's southern heritage. But at the same time, it is a major Atlantic seaport and transportation center, with diversified manufacturing activities and important air-force and navy installations.

Fall Line This "line" marks the zone where the resistant rock of the Piedmont Plateau meets the softer rock of the Coastal Plain. Rivers flowing from the plateau cut deeply into the soft rock, and as erosion lowers the surface of the plain below that of the Piedmont, waterfalls and rapids are formed. At these places, rough water necessitated a break in the boat transportation of colonial America, and settlement took place, usually on the gentler Coastal Plain. Today, cities located near the line remain as evidence of the strong influence the natural environment has upon human settlement patterns.

Land Use To state residents, South Carolina is divided into two regions. The "up country" to the north and west includes a small portion of the Blue Ridge Mountains and the hilly to rugged Piedmont Plateau. The "low country" to the south and east runs across the Atlantic Coastal Plain, gradually turning to flat, swampy tidewater and fine sand beach as it meets the Atlantic Ocean.

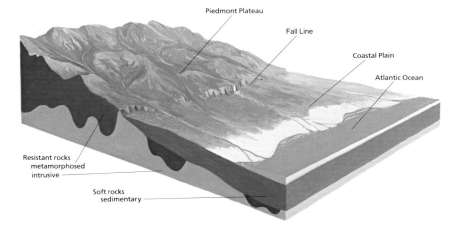

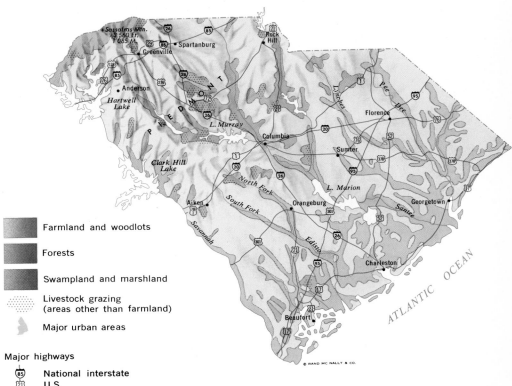

■ Farmland and woodlots

■ Forests

■ Swampland and marshland

Livestock grazing
(areas other than farmland)

Major urban areas

Major highways

National interstate

U.S.

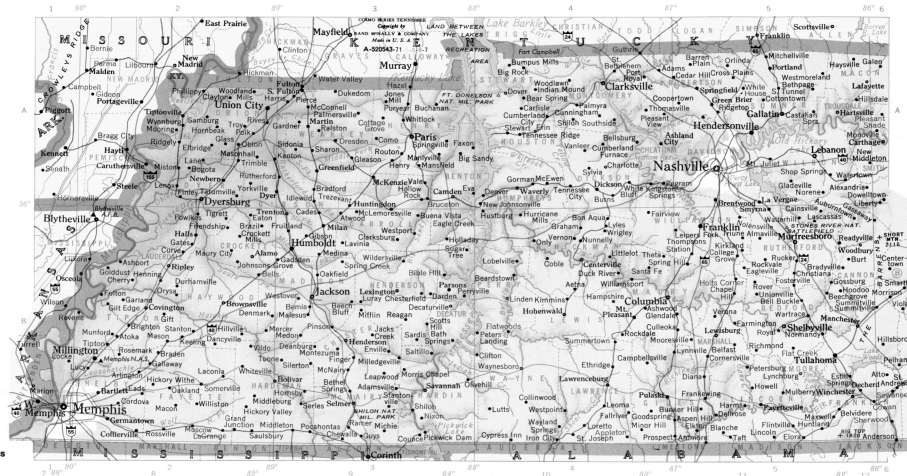

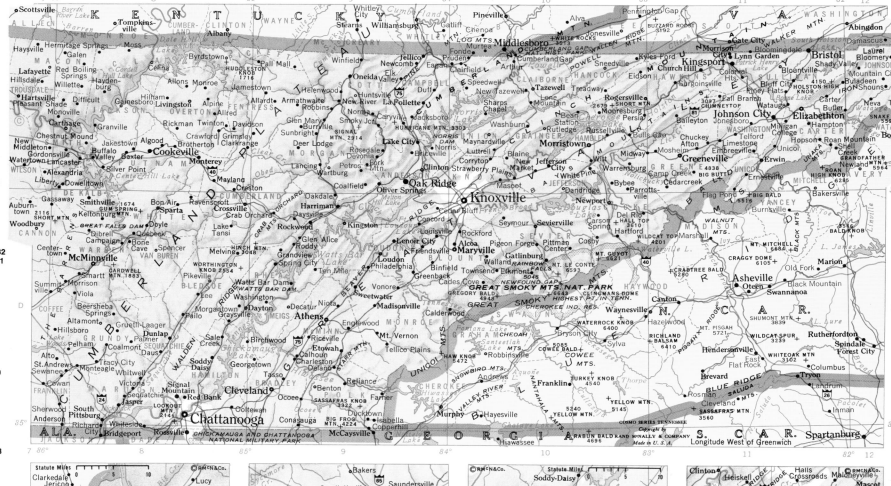

Cities and Towns

Alcoa 6,870 **D10**
Athens 12,080 **D9**
Bartlett 17,170 **B2**
Bloomingdale 9,000 **C11**
Bolivar 6,597 **B3**
Brentwood 9,431 **A5**
Bristol 23,986 **C11**
Brownsville 9,307 **B2**
Chattanooga 169,558 **D8**
Clarksville 54,777 **A4**
Cleveland 26,415 **D9**
Clinton 5,245 **C9**
Collierville 7,839 **B4**
Columbia 26,571 **B4**
Cookeville 20,535 **C8**
Covington 6,065 **B2**
Crossville 6,394 **D8**
Dayton 5,913 **D9**
Dickson 7,040 **A4**
Dyersburg 15,856 **A2**
East Ridge 21,236 **D8**
Elizabethton 12,431 **C11**
Erwin 4,739 **C11**
Fayetteville 7,559 **B5**
Franklin 12,407 **B5**
Gallatin 17,191 **A5**
Gatlinburg 3,210 **D10**
Germantown 21,482 **B2**
Greeneville 14,097 **C11**
Harriman 8,303 **D9**
Henderson 4,449 **B3**
Hendersonville 26,561 **A5**
Humboldt 10,209 **B3**
Jackson 49,131 **B3**
Jefferson City 5,612 **C10**
Johnson City 39,753 **C11**
Kingsport 32,027 **C11**
Kingston 4,441 **D9**
Knoxville 175,045 **D10**
La Follette 8,198 **C9**
Lawrenceburg 10,184 **B4**
Lebanon 11,872 **A5**
Lenoir City 5,446 **D9**
Lewisburg 8,760 **B5**
Lexington 5,934 **B3**
McKenzie 5,405 **A3**
McMinnville 10,683 **D8**
Martin 8,898 **A3**
Maryville 17,480 **D10**
Memphis 646,174 **B1**
Milan 8,083 **B3**
Millington 20,236 **B2**
Morristown 19,683 **C10**
Murfreesboro 32,845 **B5**
Nashville 455,651 **A5**
Newport 7,580 **D10**
Oak Ridge 27,662 **C9**
Paris 10,728 **A3**
Pulaski 7,184 **B4**
Red Bank 13,299 **D8**
Ripley 6,366 **B2**
Rockwood 5,767 **D9**
Savannah 6,992 **B3**
Sevierville 4,556 **D10**
Shelbyville 13,530 **B5**
Smyrna 8,839 **B5**
Soddy-Daisy 8,388 **D8**
Sparta 4,864 **D8**
Springfield 10,814 **A5**
Sweetwater 4,725 **D9**
Trenton 4,601 **B3**
Tullahoma 15,800 **B5**
Union City 10,436 **A2**
Winchester 5,821 **B5**

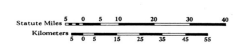

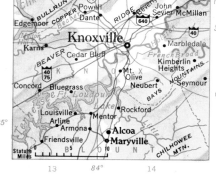

Statute Miles
Kilometers

Lambert Conformal Conic Projection
SCALE 1:1,713,000   1 Inch = 27 Statute Miles

Tennessee

POPULATION 4,899,500.
Rank: 16. *Density:* 119 people/mi²
(46 people/km²). *Urban:*
60.4%. *Rural:* 39.6%.

INCOME/CAPITA $10,893.
Rank: 38.

ENTERED UNION June 1, 1796,
16th state.

CAPITAL Nashville, 482,500.

LARGEST CITY Memphis, 671,400.

LAND AREA 41,154 mi²
(106,588 km²).
Rank: 34. *Water area:* 989 mi²
(2,561 km²).

DIMENSIONS N–S 120 miles,
E–W 430 miles.

ELEVATIONS *Highest:* Clingmans
Dome, 6,643 ft (2,025 m). *Lowest:*
Along Mississippi River, 182 ft
(55 m).

CLIMATE Hot summers; short,
generally mild winters. Moderate
rainfall, some mountain snow.

Tennessee is a pivotal region among states east of the Mississippi. It is linked culturally with the South, yet a thriving industry and one of the most extensive navigable river systems in the world tie it closely to the North.

In the 1930's, the federal government recognized the economic potential of Tennessee and decided to harness its abundant water resources to spur regional development in the area. The Tennessee Valley Authority, originally established to improve navigation, came to serve several other purposes: flood control, generation of electric power for industrial and rural needs, and conservation of land and forest resources, particularly soil ravaged by years of uncontrolled erosion. The TVA proved to be a milestone experiment that gained worldwide fame and touched off a controversy regarding federal intervention in state affairs that has yet to be resolved.

Because of the TVA and other government projects, Tennessee has developed a varied economy, producing chemicals, food products, machinery, textiles, metals, and minerals, as well as crops such as soybeans and tobacco. One of the state's primary exports, however, is electrical energy, which it supplies to some of its neighbors. Additional generators, fueled by strip-mined coal and by nuclear reactors, are adding to the state's capacity but may also be adding to its future environmental problems. The state will need to weigh carefully the benefits and liabilities of such a power network.

Tennessee's regional North-South divisions, originated in Civil War times, are still evident in the state's political and cultural life. Its eastern uplands follow northern trends, while central Tennessee allies itself with the Deep South. A region to the west shares ties with both North and South. In recent years, the Memphis metropolitan area has begun to emerge as a fourth distinct region.

Just as Tennessee's riverways have been merged into a unified network of power and navigation systems, so the state may need to find ways to unify its cultural and political regions. Whether or not this happens in the near future, Tennessee will continue to play a strong pivotal role for both its southern and northern neighbors.

Suitable rainfall and latitude account for the more than one hundred species of trees covering the Great Smoky Mountains. The range's name comes from the overhanging bluish haze, the result of hydrocarbons released by the conifer trees.

Political Affiliation Tennessee's cultural and political sectionalism between the east and the west is due partially to the state's varied landscape, which ranges from eastern mountains and central plateaus to western plains. Western terrain enabled early development of large plantations with a Southern orientation. Rugged eastern slopes dictated smaller farms and a more austere life, allied with states to the north and east. The Civil War accentuated the differences, and many easterners remained loyal to the Union even after Tennessee entered the Confederacy. Today, Northern affiliation still persists in eastern Tennessee, as reflected in its predominantly Republican voting record. The center of the state and most of the west have clung to their Democratic politics, characteristic of the Southern states.

Presidential-election results, by county

Political party
Democratic
Republican

Election year
1964 1968
1972
1976 1980

• Democratic
• Republican
• American Independent

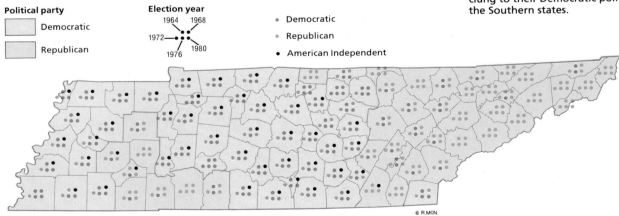

© R.MCN.

Land Use The damming of Tennessee's rivers at so many points has created a great chain of reservoirs. These long, narrow lakes along with others in neighboring states are sometimes called the Great Lakes of the South. Tennessee's reservoirs serve to control flooding and provide hydroelectric power, but they have also added another tourist attraction to the state's long list of beautiful landscapes and recreational resources.

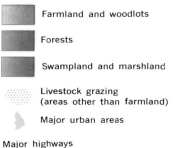

Farmland and woodlots

Forests

Swampland and marshland

Livestock grazing
(areas other than farmland)

Major urban areas

Major highways

National interstate

U.S.

Cities and Towns

Alexandria 103,217 **B5**
Annandale 35,300 **g12**
Appomattox 1,345 **C4**
Arlington 152,700 **B5**
Bedford 5,991 **C3**
Big Stone Gap 4,748 **f9**
Blacksburg 30,638 **C2**
Bluefield 5,946 **C1**
Bon Air 13,000 **C5**
Bristol 19,042 **f9**
Buena Vista 6,717 **C3**
Charlottesville 39,916 **B4**
Chesapeake 114,486 **D6**
Chester 7,000 **C5**
Chincoteague 1,607 **C7**
Christiansburg 10,345 **C2**
Clifton Forge 5,046 **C3**
Collinsville 7,400 **D3**
Colonial Heights 16,509 **C5**
Covington 9,063 **C3**
Culpepper 6,621 **B5**
Dale City 23,000 **B5**
Danville 45,642 **D3**
Emporia 4,840 **D5**
Engleside 21,400 **g12**
Fairfax 19,390 **B5**
Farmville 6,067 **C4**
Franklin 7,308 **D6**
Fredericksburg 15,322 **B5**
Front Royal 11,126 **B4**
Galax 6,524 **D2**
Hampton 122,617 **C6**
Harrisonburg 19,671 **B4**
Herndon 11,449 **B5**
Highland Springs 7,500 **C5**
Hollins 11,000 **C3**
Hopewell 23,397 **C5**
Leesburg 8,357 **A5**
Lexington 7,292 **C3**
Lynchburg 66,743 **C3**
McLean 22,000 **g12**
Manassas 15,438 **B5**
Manassas Park 6,524 **B5**
Marion 7,029 **f10**
Martinsville 18,149 **D3**
Mechanicsville 9,000 **C5**
Newport News 144,903 **D6**
Norfolk 266,979 **D6**
Norton 4,757 **f9**
Petersburg 41,055 **C5**
Poquoson 8,726 **C6**
Portsmouth 104,577 **D6**
Pulaski 10,106 **C2**
Radford 13,225 **C2**
Reston 32,000 **B5**
Richlands 5,796 **e10**
Richmond 219,214 **C5**
Roanoke 100,220 **C3**
Salem 23,958 **C2**
Shenandoah 1,861 **B4**
South Boston 7,093 **D4**
Springfield 12,500 **g12**
Staunton 21,857 **B3**
Sterling 12,000 **A5**
Suffolk 47,621 **D6**
Tazewell 4,468 **e10**
Vienna 15,469 **B5**
Vinton 8,027 **C3**
Virginia Beach 262,199 **D7**
Waynesboro 15,329 **B4**
West Springfield 16,000 **g12**
Williamsburg 9,870 **C6**
Winchester 20,217 **A4**
Woodbridge 35,000 **B5**
Wytheville 7,135 **D1**
Yorktown 390 **C6**

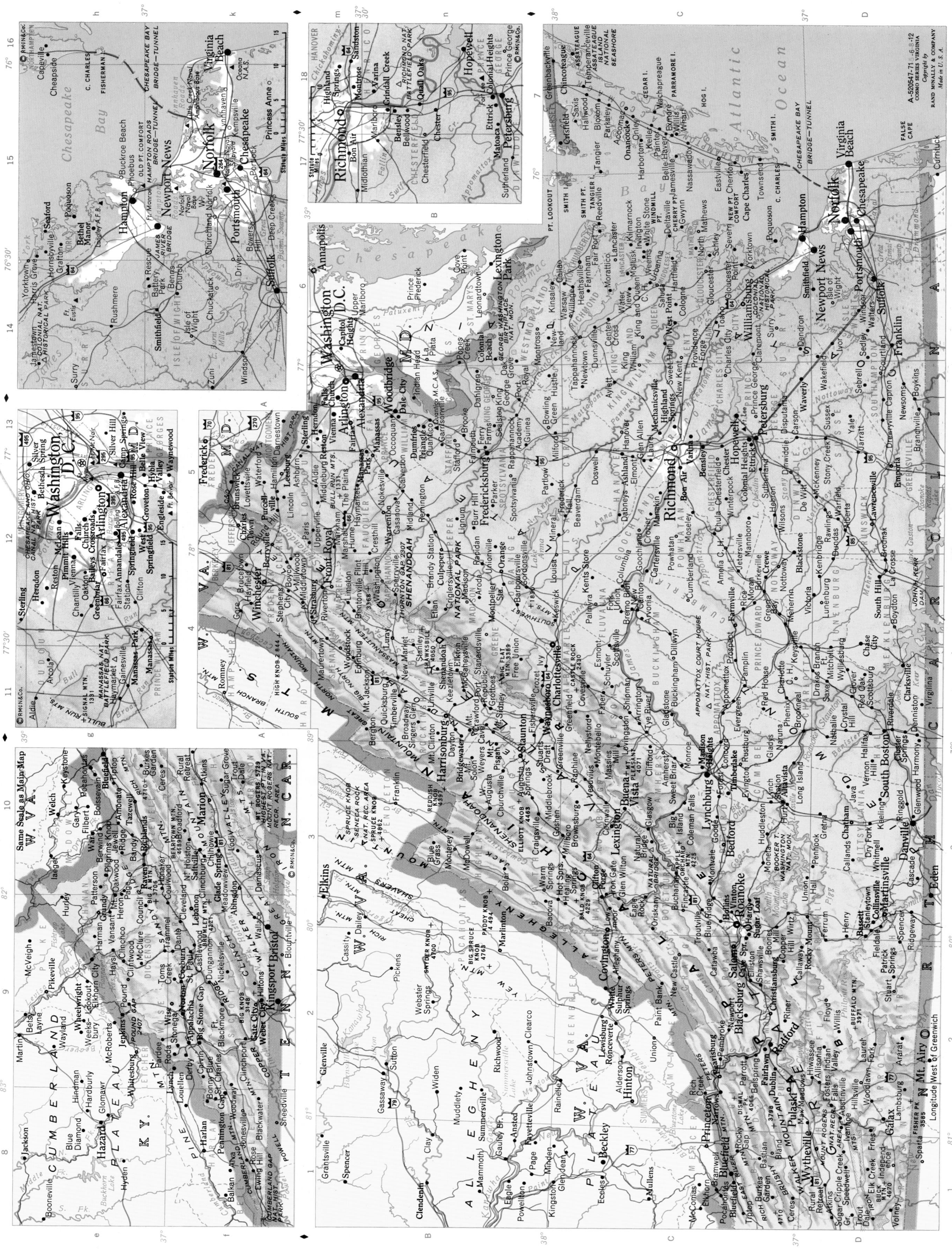

Same Scale as Major Map

Statute Miles   5 0 5 10 20 30 40
Kilometers   5 0 5 15 25 35 45 55

Lambert Conformal Conic Projection
SCALE 1:1,822,000   1 Inch = 29 Statute Miles

A-500547-71 ·6.8.12
COSMO SERIES VIRGINIA
© by Rand MᶜNally & Company
Made in U.S.A.

Virginia

POPULATION 5,943,200.
Rank: 12.*Density:* 150 people/mi²
(58 people/km²).*Urban:*
66.0%.*Rural:* 34.0%.
INCOME/CAPITA $13,584.
Rank: 12.
ENTERED UNION June 25, 1788,
10th state.

CAPITAL Richmond, 217,100.
LARGEST CITY Virginia Beach,
344,900.
LAND AREA 39,700 mi²
(102,823 km²).
Rank: 36.*Water area:* 1,063 mi²
(2,753 km²).
DIMENSIONS N–S 205 miles,
E–W 425 miles.

ELEVATIONS *Highest:* Mount
Rogers, 5,729 ft
(1,746 m).*Lowest:* Atlantic Ocean
shoreline, sea level.
CLIMATE Hot summers, short
winters with some snow.
Moderate rainfall.

In leadership, Virginia has no equal. Time and again, the forces of American history have called upon the state's citizens to face extraordinary challenges in peace and war. No other state has been the birthplace of so many presidents—eight in all. During the Revolutionary and Civil wars, Virginia was often torn by battle, its countryside scarred by the action of opposing armies. Yet it also served as the site of peace. The Revolutionary War ended at Yorktown, and Lee surrendered to Grant at Appomattox, not far from the Confederate capital in Richmond.

Virginia today still plays an important role in America's political leadership. The nation's capital lies just beyond the border to the northeast, and Virginia is one of Washington, D.C.'s, main support areas, supplying much of its work force and housing numerous government agencies. Government is a major industry in the state.

Virginia has also shown its leadership in meeting the challenges of a changing modern economy. Although no longer the great domain it was in colonial times, when its borders included West Virginia, the state is still rich in resources. Agriculture remains an important part of the state's economy, and since World War II, manufacturing has increased. Additional revenues come from a tourist industry attracted by the state's historical sites and picturesque landscapes.

Virginia continues to face new and demanding challenges that will once again tap its traditional leadership capacities. At one time a largely rural state, Virginia is now the southern anchor of the great urban-industrial corridor stretching north to Boston. Not only does this place the state in a strategic position with respect to the North, but because Virginia still identifies strongly with the South, it makes Virginia a pivot between northern and southern industrial states. And the state's proximity to the nation's capital will continue to cast it in a position of national leadership. Virginia will need to manage these and future roles carefully to maintain the high quality of natural and social environments for which it has always been known.

Virginia is rich in natural beauty as well as history. The heavily forested Blue Ridge Mountains that cross the state are part of the Appalachians and separate the Piedmont region from Virginia's Great Valley. In addition to being a major tourist attraction, the mountains contain traces of another side of America's past, different from that recalled by the colonial and Civil War landmarks found elsewhere in the state. Many of the homes and small subsistence farms of the mountain people display the country's pioneer heritage, employing farming and building techniques passed down from generation to generation.

Historic Virginia From the first permanent English settlement at Jamestown to the battlefields of the Revolutionary and Civil wars, the history of the United States can be traced within the boundaries of Virginia. The state is the site of many of the most important events in the country's development, and the presidents' homes, restored buildings, and other landmarks reflect the leadership role Virginia has often played.

Arlington National Cemetery
Alexandria
Manassas National Battlefield Park (Bull Run)
Mount Vernon
Gunston Hall
New Market Battlefield Park
Fredericksburg
George Washington Birthplace National Monument
Staunton
Charlottesville
Lexington
Richmond
Appomattox Court House National Historical Park
Berkeley Plantation
Williamsburg
Yorktown
Jamestown
Booker T. Washington National Monument
Norfolk
Cape Henry Memorial and Lighthouse
Cumberland Gap National Historical Park
Abingdon
Danville

© R.MCN.

Farmland and woodlots

Forests

Swampland and marshland

Livestock grazing (areas other than farmland)

Major urban areas

Major highways
95 National interstate
U.S.

Land Use Virginia's land is productive as well as scenic, and much of the state's history is based on its tobacco crop. Although the state's farming has become increasingly diversified over the years, tobacco ranks as the second-greatest contributor to state agricultural wealth. Dairy farming, however, now provides Virginia with more income.

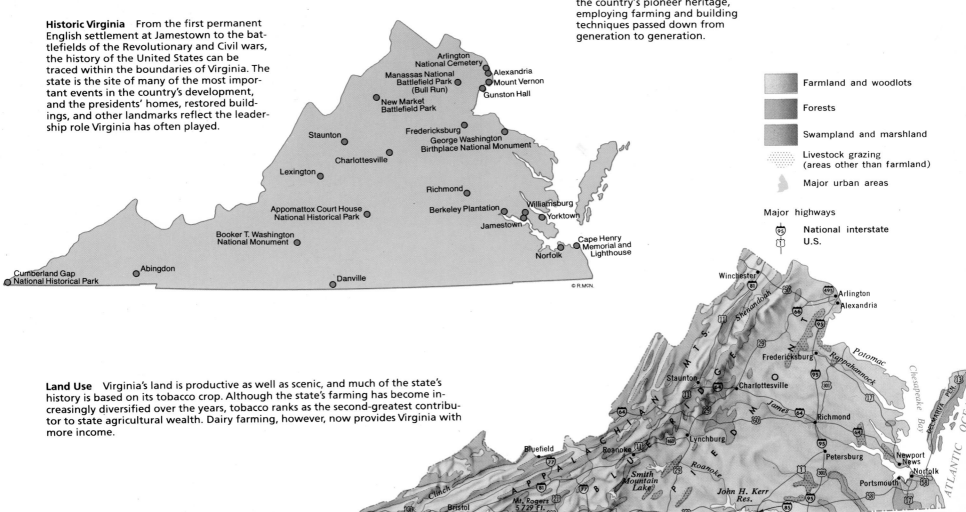

Winchester
Arlington
Alexandria
Shenandoah
Fredericksburg
Rappahannock
Potomac
Staunton
Charlottesville
James
Richmond
Chesapeake Bay
DELMARVA PEN.
Bluefield
Roanoke
Lynchburg
Petersburg
Newport News
Norfolk
Smith Mountain Lake
Roanoke
John H. Kerr Res.
Portsmouth
ATLANTIC OCEAN
Clinch
Mt. Rogers 5,729 Ft. 1,746 M.
Bristol
Danville
© RAND MCNALLY & CO.

Cities and Towns

Barboursville 2,871 **C2**
Beckley 20,492 **D3**
Bluefield 16,060 **D3**
Bridgeport 6,604 **B4**
Buckhannon 6,820 **C4**
Charleston 63,968 **C3**
Charles Town 2,857 **B7**
Chesapeake 2,364 **C3**
Chester 3,297 **A4**
Clarksburg 22,371 **B4**
Cross Lanes 3,500 **C3**
Dunbar 9,285 **m12**
Elkins 8,536 **C5**
Fairmont 23,863 **B4**
Fayetteville 2,366 **C3**
Follansbee 3,994 **A4**
Gary 2,233 **D3**
Grafton 6,845 **B4**
Harpers Ferry 361 **B7**
Hinton 4,622 **D4**
Huntington 63,684 **C2**
Hurricane 3,751 **C2**
Kenova 4,454 **C2**
Keyser 6,569 **B6**
Kingwood 2,877 **B5**
Lewisburg 3,065 **D4**
Logan 3,029 **D3**
McMechen 2,402 **B4**
Madison 3,228 **C3**
Mannington 3,036 **B4**
Martinsburg 13,063 **B7**
Montgomery 3,104 **C3**
Moorefield 2,257 **B6**
Morgantown 27,605 **B5**
Moundsville 12,419 **B4**
Mullens 2,919 **D3**
New Martinsville 7,109 **B4**
Nitro 8,074 **C3**
Oak Hill 7,120 **D3**
Oceana 2,143 **D3**
Paden City 3,671 **B4**
Parkersburg 39,967 **B3**
Petersburg 2,084 **C5**
Philippi 3,194 **B4**
Point Pleasant 5,682 **C2**
Princeton 7,493 **D3**
Rand 2,500 **C3**
Ranson 2,471 **B7**
Ravenswood 4,126 **C3**
Richwood 3,568 **C4**
Ripley 3,464 **C3**
Romney 2,094 **B6**
Ronceverte 2,312 **D4**
St. Albans 12,402 **C3**
St. Marys 2,219 **B3**
Salem 2,706 **B4**
Shinnston 3,059 **B4**
Sistersville 2,367 **B4**
South Charleston 15,968 **C3**
Spencer 2,799 **C3**
Stonewood 2,058 **k10**
Summersville 2,972 **C4**
Tyler Heights 3,200 **C3**
Vienna 11,618 **B3**
War 2,158 **D3**
Weirton 25,371 **A4**
Welch 3,885 **D3**
Wellsburg 3,963 **A4**
Weston 6,250 **B4**
Westover 4,884 **B5**
Wheeling 43,070 **A4**
White Sulphur Springs 3,371 **D4**
Williamson 5,219 **D2**
Williamstown 3,095 **B3**

Statute Miles 5 0 5 10 20 30 40
Kilometers 5 0 5 15 25 35 45 55

Lambert Conformal Conic Projection
SCALE 1:1,704,000 1 Inch = 27 Statute Miles

West Virginia

POPULATION 1,934,600.
Rank: 34.*Density:* 80 people/mi²
(31 people/km²).*Urban:*
36.2%.*Rural:* 63.8%.
INCOME/CAPITA $9,763.
Rank: 48.
ENTERED UNION June 20, 1863,
35th state.

CAPITAL Charleston, 57,500.
LARGEST CITY Charleston.
LAND AREA 24,124 mi²
(62,481 km²).
Rank: 41.*Water area:* 112 mi²
(290 km²).
DIMENSIONS N–S 200 miles,
E–W 225 miles.

ELEVATIONS *Highest:* Spruce Knob,
4,863 ft (1,482 m).*Lowest:* Along
Potomac River, 240 ft (73 m).
CLIMATE Hot summers in valleys,
mild in mountains; cool winters.
Ample rainfall.

After more than one hundred years of statehood, West Virginia seems to be on the verge of coming into its own. For years, despite a wide variety of natural resources, its mountainous terrain has contributed to problems of a poor economy and high unemployment. Yet just as the events of history and the state's to-pography have sometimes worked against West Virginia, the deter-mined efforts of its people coupled with current economic trends and modern transportation systems promise a brighter future.

West Virginia's terrain has long played a major role in determining the economy and culture of the state. It was once part of Virginia, a vast state stretching from the Atlantic Ocean to the Ohio River. But the mountainous terrain of western Virginia led to the development of an economy based on small-scale farming and industry, differing markedly from the wealthy plantation culture of the eastern part of the state. Western Virginia's growing demand for statehood was rein-forced by the area's North-tending sympathies at the outset of the Civil War, and in 1863, the region gained statehood as West Virginia.

But the state found itself outside many of the economic trends that followed. West Virginia is one of the most mountainous states in the country, fragmented into small, isolated valleys that make com-munication and trade among villages and towns difficult. With few areas flat enough for extensive agriculture, regions available for cul-tivation could support only subsistence farming, an activity of little importance in the national economy. Although coal, natural gas, oil, and high-grade sand used in glassmaking were available for devel-opment, rugged terrain made transportation difficult, and growth in these industries was therefore limited. With the advent of mecha-nized coal mining and strip-mining, many workers found themselves out of a job.

But much of this is in the past. Today, state boundaries are less important in defining growth and decline, and transportation sys-tems connect West Virginia with surrounding states and the nation. In addition, years of outmigration by the unemployed mean that industrial growth can more readily raise the standard of living. After years of living in the shadow of its more prosperous neighbors, West Virginia is at last emerging as a strong, developing region on its own.

Site of abolitionist John Brown's armory raid and a frequent battleground during the Civil War, Harpers Ferry reflects one side of the many conflicts between eastern and western Virginia that eventually led to West Virginia's independent statehood.

Settlement Patterns West Virginia's mountain-and-valley landscape exhibits the limitations the land imposes, with settlement concentrated in the more-level Kanawha Valley. And whereas growth usually means widespread population dis-tribution, West Virginia's terrain continues to inhibit the urban sprawl found in many other states.

Extent of urbanization

≡ 1935 ||||| Additional as of 1976

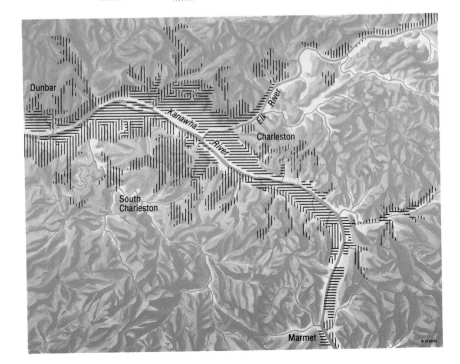

Land Use West Virginia's irregular shape is matched by those patches of land suitable for agriculture, industry, and urban growth. Valley bottomland is usually of greatest value to farmers, who profit from the rich soils deposited by rivers, and to industrialists, who take advantage of river transportation.

Farmland and woodlots

Forests

Livestock grazing (areas other than farmland)

Major urban areas

Major highways

🛡 77 National interstate
🛡 19 U.S.

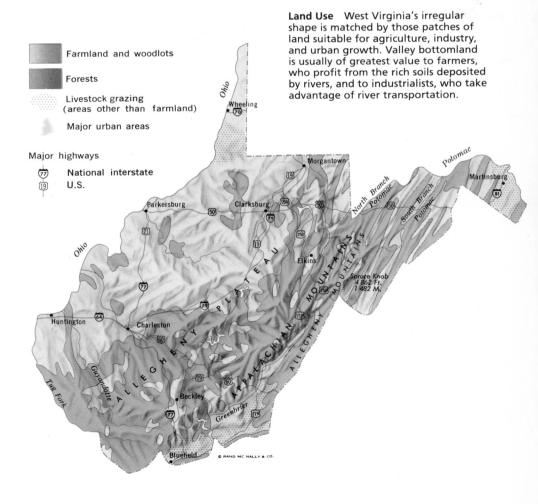

CORNFIELD EDGE / IOWA

The Heartland

The Heartland

Power from the Earth Abundant

WHAT IS THE HEARTLAND? IT IS TRACTORS growling across the broad fields. It is a robot welding an automobile frame. It is also children gathering arrowheads in dozens of places where Native Americans once ruled the territory. It is unearthing prehistoric skeletons, hiking in the wilderness, poking among the ashes of ancient volcanic formations, or observing a wide variety of wildlife. Reclaimed and preserved, much of the Heartland is as it was 150 or more years ago.

The face of the Heartland is mostly open and green, refusing to flaunt an imperious countenance. The land rolls along on flats and knolls. Small streams and rivers curl like commas around the fertile bottoms. The once-dense forests are preserved mostly in state and national forests — of which there are many — and by a few conservationist owners who value maple, oak, ash, and poplar more than they value annual cash crops.

The Heartland has no ocean coastline, but water and waterways have been important to its development. Its eastern half is almost completely surrounded by navigable waters. In addition to the Great Lakes, which contain half of the fresh water in the world, there exists a network of major rivers and their tributaries, which provided access to the unmapped frontiers and, later, became the arteries of communications and commerce.

The main artery of transport, the Mississippi River, splices the whole nation together, draining thirty-one states and two Canadian provinces. Its watershed stretches from the Allegheny Mountains to the Rockies. At its source — the clear waters of Lake Itasca in northern Minnesota — the Mississippi is ten to twelve feet wide and two feet deep. It runs northward for a short span, then twists and turns toward the southeast. Approaching the Twin Cities, Minneapolis and St. Paul, it collects itself between high bluffs, grows deeper and wider, and becomes navigable for commercial boats.

In Missouri, the river has left its mark in the bluffs and limestone caverns. They were formed by groundwater holding carbon dioxide and organic acids, which ate into the limestone at its fracture lines. The bluffs, caves, and limestone escarpments end at Cape Girardeau in southern Missouri. At Cairo,

Illinois
Indiana
Iowa
Kansas
Michigan
Minnesota
Missouri
Nebraska
North Dakota
Ohio
South Dakota
Wisconsin

Illinois, the Father of Waters, in company with the Ohio River, forms a vast and restless floodplain reaching to New Orleans.

The Heartland is half agricultural and half industrial, but the cities grew out of the agriculture surrounding them. Ohio, Michigan, Wisconsin, Illinois, and Indiana, all lying in the curving industrial corridor around the Great Lakes, are generally considered industrial. But they are also agricultural. Illinois, for example, produces more grain and legumes than Iowa, although Iowa leads all Heartland states in livestock production. The northern tier—Michigan, Wisconsin, and Minnesota—also produces food in abundance, in spite of a shorter growing season. Minnesota is third among the Heartland states in livestock production.

These three states are also ruggedly attractive, with their lakes, hills, and tall timber. Minnesota, the Land of 10,000 Lakes, actually has more than 15,000 lakes. Not far behind are Michigan with 11,000 and Wisconsin with 8,500.

The nation's wheat capital, Kansas, also sits in the Heartland, where it produces a fifth of the total crop in the United States. South Dakota produces grain, too, but mostly in the "east river" area set off by the Missouri River. Oats, flax, and hay also grow well.

Farther west, the low mountains called the Black Hills nudge Wyoming. They are "black" because, viewed from the distant plain, their domed forests appear invitingly dark. Wild animals thrive here. The land was once the bottom of an inland sea, where subsequent glaciers ironed out plains and prairies, gouged tranquil lakes and rivers, and heaved up the Badlands. The fossils they have given up document the world of dinosaurs and other prehistoric animals. This area is also the nation's largest supplier of gold.

Today, one can still go from the prevailing openness of the farmland into the coolness and mystery of the woods, where all things grow in haphazard beauty instead of in the neat and ordered rows of the tilled land. There is a harmonizing of the tame and the wild in these woods and pastures: smooth and rounded slopes, jagged gullies, short mowed meadows, and scruffy wild grass. The sunlight, so harsh on the cultivated rows, falls softened and gracious in the open spaces in the woods.

Overleaf– EAGLE ROCK, SCOTTS BLUFF NATIONAL MONUMENT / NEBRASKA

Below– NIOBRARA RIVER, AGATE FOSSIL BEDS NATIONAL MONUMENT / NEBRASKA

Above– OHIO RIVER AT POWHATAN POINT / OHIO

ST. CROIX RIVER DALLES, INTERSTATE PARK / MINNESOTA-WISCONSIN

Top– PRAIRIE'S EDGE, BADLANDS NATIONAL PARK / SOUTH DAKOTA

Bottom– BIG SPRING, CURRENT RIVER, OZARK NATIONAL SCENIC RIVERWAYS / MISSOURI

Right– LITTLE MISSOURI RIVER COUNTRY, THEODORE ROOSEVELT NATIONAL PARK / NORTH DAKOTA

Left– MAPLE AND BIRCH, VOYAGEURS NATIONAL PARK / MINNESOTA

Right– MINER'S CASTLE, LAKE SUPERIOR, PICTURED ROCKS NATIONAL LAKESHORE / MICHIGAN

FARM ROAD NEAR GALENA / ILLINOIS

MITCHELL PASS, OREGON TRAIL, SCOTTS BLUFF NATIONAL MONUMENT / NEBRASKA

Left– MOONRISE, CHIMNEY ROCK NATIONAL HISTORIC SITE / NEBRASKA

Below– MOONRISE, MONUMENT ROCKS / KANSAS

Maps of the Heartland...The Midwest

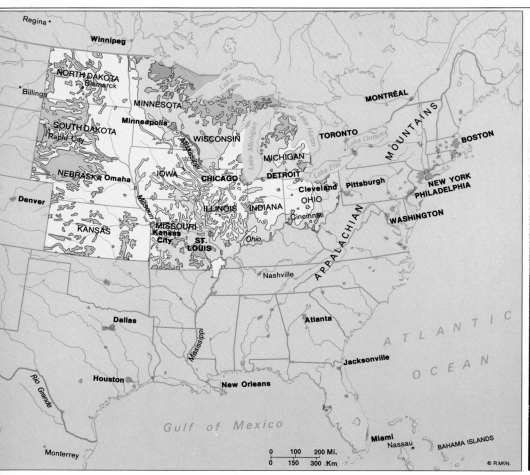

Land Use The Midwest embodies the agricultural-industrial nature of the American economy, and this dual role is reflected in the region's land use. Dominating the area is an almost continuous expanse of some of the most productive farmland in the world. And this agricultural landscape is dotted with many of the country's most important urban-industrial centers—among them Chicago, Detroit, St. Louis, and Cleveland. Northern areas contribute to the lumber industry, and forests are the principal land feature.

While nature divides the land in asymmetrical patterns, Americans rarely do; this geometric patchwork of cropland in southern Minnesota exemplifies human division of the midwestern landscape. However, regularly spaced farmsteads, cities, and roads did not develop at random. They are, instead, the result of the rectangular survey system, which was ideally suited for the relatively flat land of the Midwest. In this way, the government divided the area into right-angled parcels for settlement.

The Mississippi River played a major role in the development of the Midwest. This easily navigated transportation route was first a catalyst to settlement of the region and now continues to provide a low-cost shipping route to national and international markets. As the river flows to the Gulf of Mexico, St. Louis, shown here, is the last of the major midwestern cities through which it passes.

The Midwest leads a double life as one of the richest agricultural regions in the world and a diversified industrial center of almost unsurpassed capacity. The Midwest could easily comprise two separate, enviably productive nations, one agricultural and the other industrial, if the two activities could be separated territorially. But they overlap spatially, and their interests are inextricably entwined. Concentrations of agriculture or heavy-manufacturing activities do exist, but highly productive farmland often abuts a city, and skilled machinists and manufacturing plants are dispersed among small agriculturally based towns.

Nineteenth-century Americans recognized the Midwest's potential, and states such as Ohio, Indiana, and Illinois were quickly formed as people moved west over the Appalachian Mountains. More ingenuity was required as migrants approached the Midwest's western margin, a semiarid zone with a fragile environment, once known as the Great American Desert. That this description proved inappropriate testifies to the resourcefulness of the settlers and to the Midwest's advantageous natural situation.

The Midwest's natural assets include its climate, waterways, mineral resources, and soils. The penetration of the Gulf of Mexico into the North American continent and the lack of mountain ranges in the Southeast allow moist air masses from the Gulf to flow north, supplying the Midwest with precipitation. The waterways of the Great Lakes and St. Lawrence Seaway and the Mississippi, Missouri, and Ohio rivers endow the area with one of the best natural transportation systems in the world, allowing access to the Atlantic Ocean and the Gulf of Mexico. Thousands of years of glacial attrition and deposition have also left the region with accessible deposits of metal ores and rich soils.

Because of these excellent soils, agribusiness is of major importance to all Midwest states. However, no state escapes the conflict resulting

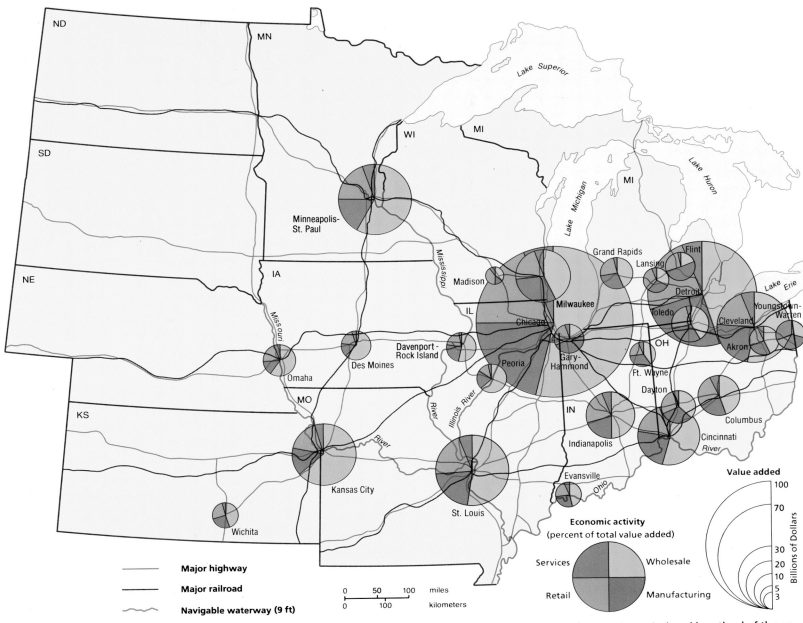

Major highway

Major railroad

Navigable waterway (9 ft)

© R.MCN.

0   50   100   miles
0   100   kilometers

Value added

100
70
30
20
10
5
3

Billions of Dollars

Economic activity
(percent of total value added)

Services   Wholesale

Retail   Manufacturing

Agricultural-Industrial Giant   The Midwest is the agricultural heartland of the nation, containing over forty percent of its farms and producing much of its income from agriculture. Although more than half of the land is considered cropland, the majority of the Midwest's population lives in urban centers. These cities contribute one-third of the nation's manufacturing and over twenty-five percent of its wholesale, its retail, and its shopping trade. Centrally located with access to transportation routes, the region plays a major role in national and international trade.

from competition between rural-agricultural and urban-industrial interests. This conflict is especially pronounced in Illinois, where the "Downstate" area and Chicago vie unceasingly.

The Midwest is sometimes viewed as the region where national political opinions and marketing trends can be most readily fathomed, but this is a role the region plays with hesitancy. Inasmuch as the Midwest best represents agriculture and diversified industry, the two activities that have long defined the nation's strength, it could be considered a microcosm of the country's economy. However, it would be a mistake to accept this as a sign of regional homogeneity in social outlook and political belief. On the contrary, the Midwest is a region where varying opinions are expressed and defended. Wide differences of opinion might, in fact, be seen as a hallmark of midwestern government, and this region has a history of launching both progressive and conservative movements and politicians into the political arena.

A hundred years ago, the Midwest was one of the most glamourous and rapidly growing regions in the nation. Today, it is occasionally maligned as an area with problems stemming from its changing agricultural techniques and its long industrial history. The Midwest's rural population has been moving to the cities, and many people have been leaving the region altogether for western and southern states.

Despite its problems, the Midwest still has great potential. Its transportation systems provide easy access to vast resources and markets, and the region has retained a large, skilled labor force. Today, the midwestern states continue to diversify industrially as they seek to attract more high-technology and service industries. In adapting to current situations and keeping up with national trends, the Midwest is carrying on its tradition of resourcefulness. Against the background of excellent human and natural resources, this resilience will most likely ensure the region's success in the coming decades.

Grain Shipment   The Midwest acts as a grain supplier to the world, and shipments indicate the response of this extraordinary granary to international needs. Rich soils, level-to-rolling terrain, an adequate growing season, and plentiful water supplies characterize the Midwest's agricultural endowment. For maximum production, farmers employ highly mechanized systems of commercial agriculture. And even government programs to curtail production to cut surpluses do not succeed; vast quantities of grain are shipped to ports annually.

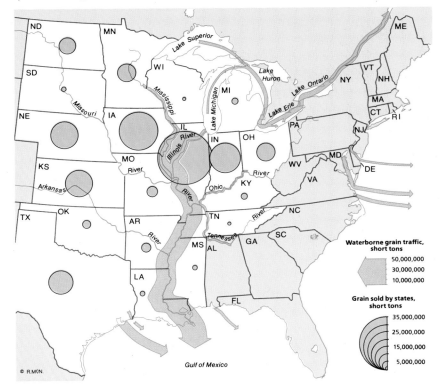

Waterborne grain traffic, short tons

50,000,000
30,000,000
10,000,000

Grain sold by states, short tons

35,000,000
25,000,000
15,000,000
5,000,000

© R.MCN.   Gulf of Mexico

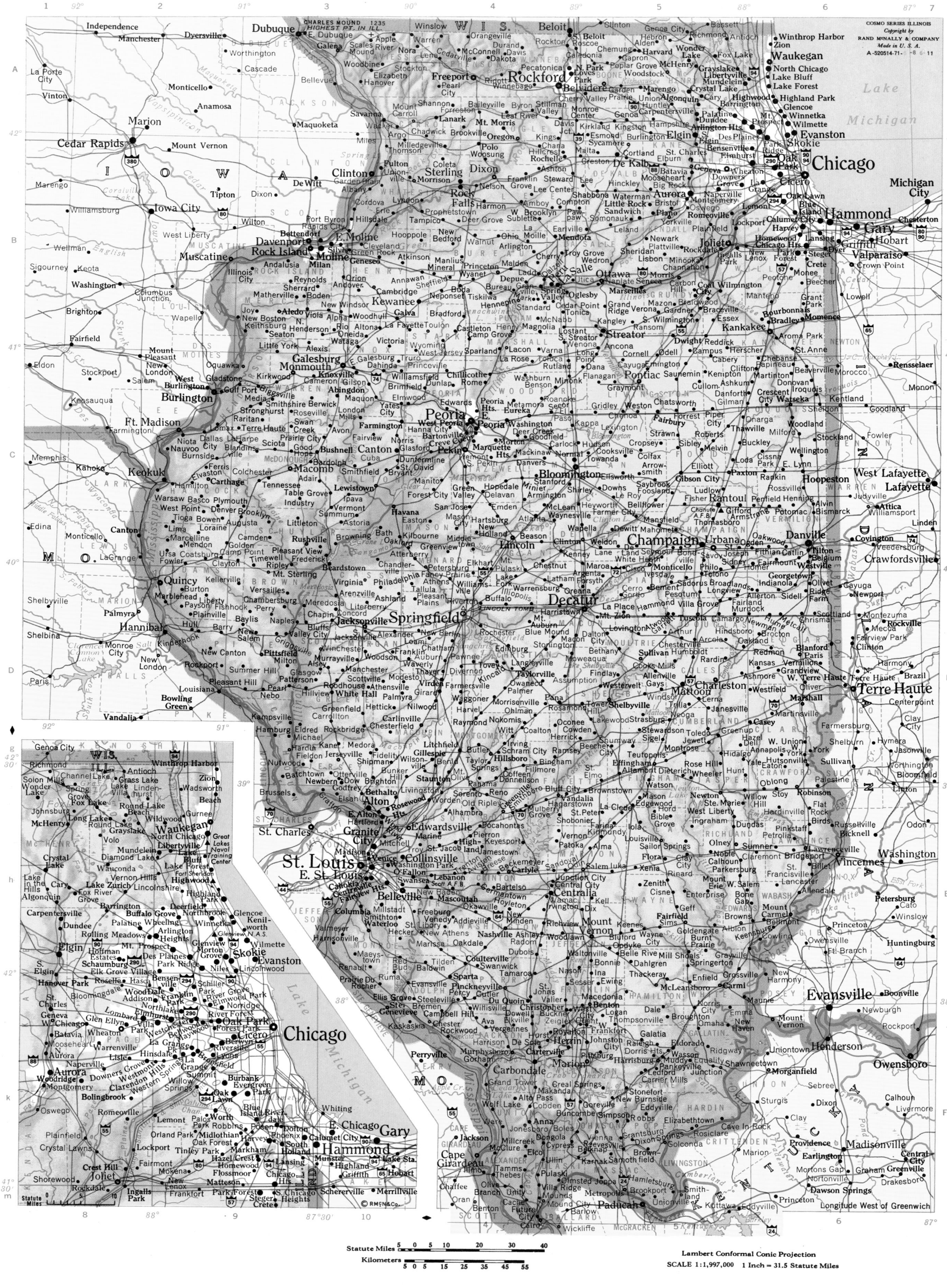

COSMO SERIES ILLINOIS
Copyright by
RAND McNALLY & COMPANY
Made in U. S. A.
A-520514-71- -8 6-11

Cities and Towns

Alton 34,171 E3
Arlington Heights 66,116 A5
Aurora 81,293 B5
Belleville 41,580 E4
Berwyn 46,849 k9
Bloomington 44,189 C4
Bourbonnais 13,280 B6
Brookfield 19,395 k9
Cahokia 18,904 E3
Cairo 5,931 F4
Calumet City 39,697 B6
Canton 14,626 C3
Carbondale 26,414 F4
Centralia 15,126 E4
Champaign 58,133 C5
Charleston 19,355 D5
Chicago 3,005,072 B6
Cicero 61,232 B6
Danville 38,985 C6
Decatur 94,081 D5
De Kalb 33,099 B5
Des Plaines 53,568 A6
Dixon 15,701 B4
Downers Grove 42,572 B5
East St. Louis 55,200 E3
Elgin 63,981 A5
Elmhurst 44,276 B6
Evanston 73,706 A6
Freeport 26,266 A4
Galena 3,876 A3
Galesburg 35,305 C3
Granite City 36,815 E3
Gurnee 7,179 h9
Highland Park 30,611 A6
Jacksonville 20,284 D3
Joliet 77,956 B5
Kankakee 30,141 B6
Kewanee 14,508 B4
Lake Forest 15,245 A6
La Salle 10,347 B4
Lincoln 16,327 C4
Lombard 36,897 k8
Macomb 19,863 C3
Marion 14,031 F5
Mattoon 19,055 D5
Moline 46,278 B3
Monmouth 10,706 C3
Mount Prospect 52,634 A6
Mount Vernon 17,193 E5
Nauvoo 1,133 C2
Normal 35,672 C5
North Chicago 38,774 A6
Oak Lawn 60,590 B6
Oak Park 54,887 B6
Ottawa 18,166 B5
Pekin 33,967 C4
Peoria 124,160 C4
Peru 10,886 B4
Pontiac 11,227 C5
Quincy 42,554 D2
Rockford 139,712 A4
Rock Island 46,928 B3
Salem 7,813 E5
Schaumburg 53,305 h8
Skokie 60,278 A6
Springfield 100,054 D4
Sterling 16,281 B4
Streator 14,795 B5
Taylorville 11,386 D4
Urbana 35,978 C5
Vandalia 5,338 E4
Waukegan 67,653 A6
Wheaton 43,043 B5
Zion 17,861 A6

Statute Miles 5 5 10 20 30 40
Kilometers 5 0 5 15 25 35 55

Lambert Conformal Conic Projection
SCALE 1:1,997,000 1 Inch = 31.5 Statute Miles

Longitude West of Greenwich

CHARLES MOUND 1235
HIGHEST PT. IN ILL.

Illinois

POPULATION 11,657,600.
Rank: 6. *Density:* 209 people/mi²
(81 people/km²). *Urban:*
83.3%. *Rural:* 16.7%.
INCOME/CAPITA $14,115.
Rank: 9.
ENTERED UNION Dec. 3, 1818,
21st state.

CAPITAL Springfield, 102,500.
LARGEST CITY Chicago, 3,021,700.
LAND AREA 55,646 mi²
(144,122 km²).
Rank: 24. *Water area:* 2,226 mi²
(5,765 km²).
DIMENSIONS N–S 380 miles,
E–W 205 miles.

ELEVATIONS *Highest:* Charles
Mound, 1,235 ft (376 m). *Lowest:*
Along Mississippi River, 279 ft
(85 m).
CLIMATE Cold winters, hot
summers; moderate rainfall.

Illinois, one of the nation's wealthiest states, is also one of the most clearly divided, reflecting more than any of its neighbors the great division between industry and agriculture in the midwestern economy. In fact, Illinois may be regarded almost as two states. The first, based on manufacturing, is centered on the Chicago metropolitan area and other northern cities. Here, communities are often split between urban and suburban areas, among racial and ethnic groups, and between rich and poor—divisions deeply rooted in the state's history and difficult to overcome. The second "state," founded on agriculture and known as downstate, is made up of a central agricultural area and a southern region rich in coal.

Despite these regional differences, Illinois has played a vital role in the Midwest and in the nation. It leads almost all other states in many sectors of manufacturing, agriculture, and mining. Chicago has served as the transportation hub of the nation since the nineteenth century. Its railroads, water traffic, and highways have adapted easily to twentieth-century technology; and O'Hare Airport, outside of Chicago, is widely acknowledged as the busiest air terminal in the world. With access to both the Great Lakes and the Mississippi waterways, and with nationwide rail and road connections, Illinois is ideally suited to gather resources, process them, and distribute finished products throughout the country.

Yet now, in the face of a changing economy, the deep divisions in Illinois are exacting a toll that may affect the future welfare of the state. Traditionally, regional and local interests have been set above the concerns of the state as a whole, and such partisanship has led to political fragmentation. As a result, Illinois is split into more units of government and elects more officials than any other state. In addition, the conflict between Chicago and downstate is marked by a continual tug-of-war over revenues and political influence. Such divisions make integration of statewide policies particularly difficult, and the refusal to compromise could have serious, long-term consequences. In response, officials and other citizens in the two "states" are working to unify Illinois into one commonwealth that will be able to meet the needs of its people and face the challenges of the future.

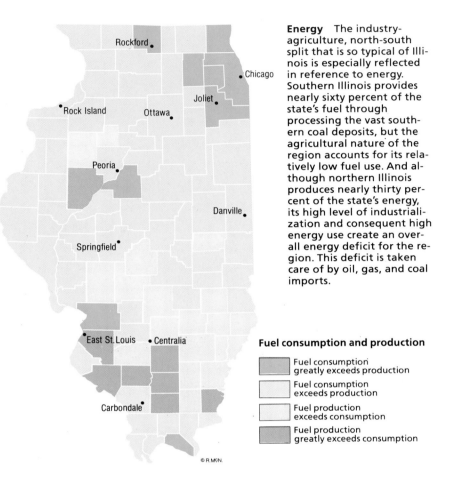

Energy The industry-agriculture, north-south split that is so typical of Illinois is especially reflected in reference to energy. Southern Illinois provides nearly sixty percent of the state's fuel through processing the vast southern coal deposits, but the agricultural nature of the region accounts for its relatively low fuel use. And although northern Illinois produces nearly thirty percent of the state's energy, its high level of industrialization and consequent high energy use create an overall energy deficit for the region. This deficit is taken care of by oil, gas, and coal imports.

Fuel consumption and production

Fuel consumption greatly exceeds production

Fuel consumption exceeds production

Fuel production exceeds consumption

Fuel production greatly exceeds consumption

© R. McN.

Land Use Illinois's rich, level soils have always guaranteed a productive agriculture. This is true with respect to all the feed and grain crops and meat, dairy, and poultry products for which the Midwest is famous. But besides its environmental resources, Illinois's location between the Great Lakes and the Mississippi River system has made the state a center of transportation for the nation, assuring the rapid growth of state cities and industry. In turn, urban and industrial areas are concentrated where water, rail, road, and air connections meet.

Farmland (cropland and pastureland)

Farmland and woodlots

Swampland and marshland

Livestock grazing (areas other than farmland)

Major urban areas

Major highways

80 National interstate

66 U.S.

© RAND McNALLY & CO.

The success of Illinois is largely dependent upon Chicago. A manufacturing center, the city contributes greatly to the state's income, and its location provides access to the transportation routes necessary for profitable industry and agriculture. But just as Illinois depends upon Chicago, so does Chicago depend upon the rest of the state. Resources found in other areas provide much of the input that keeps the city's factories productive. And the state's agriculture helps make Chicago an agribusiness and finance center: many crops and much of the livestock raised in other parts of the state are bought and sold through the Chicago Board of Trade.

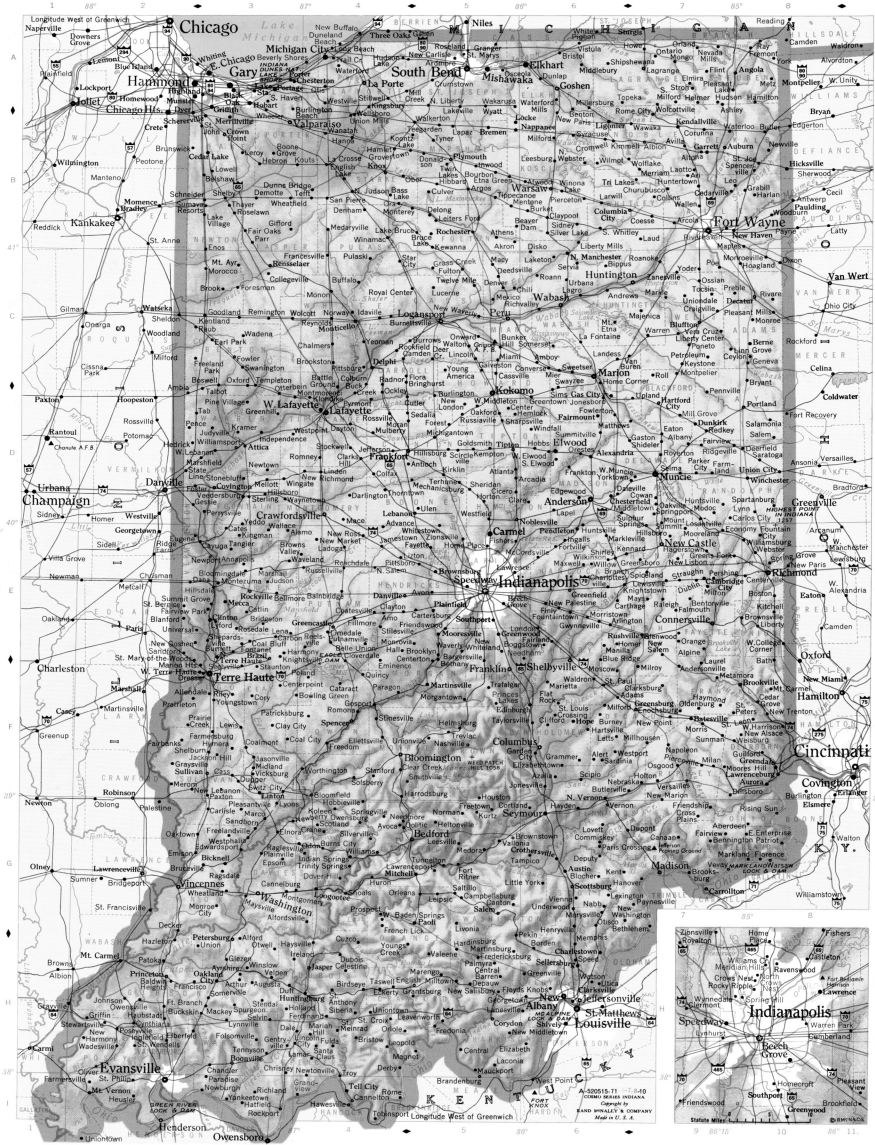

Cities and Towns

Anderson 64,695 **D6**
Auburn 8,122 **B7**
Bedford 14,410 **G5**
Beech Grove 13,196 **E5**
Bloomington 52,044 **F4**
Bluffton 8,705 **C7**
Brazil 7,852 **E3**
Carmel 18,272 **E5**
Clarksville 15,164 **H6**
Columbus 30,614 **F6**
Connersville 17,023 **E7**
Corydon 2,724 **H5**
Crawfordsville 13,325 **D4**
Crown Point 16,455 **B3**
Decatur 8,649 **C8**
East Chicago 39,786 **A3**
Elkhart 41,305 **A6**
Elwood 10,867 **D6**
Evansville 130,496 **I2**
Fort Wayne 172,028 **B7**
Frankfort 15,168 **D4**
Franklin 11,563 **F5**
French Lick 2,265 **G4**
Gary 151,953 **A3**
Goshen 19,665 **A6**
Greencastle 8,403 **E4**
Greensburg 9,254 **F7**
Greenwood 19,327 **E5**
Griffith 17,026 **A3**
Hammond 93,714 **A2**
Highland 25,935 **A3**
Hobart 22,987 **A3**
Huntington 16,202 **C7**
Indianapolis 700,807 **E5**
Jasper 9,097 **H4**
Jeffersonville 21,220 **H6**
Kokomo 47,808 **D5**
Lafayette 43,011 **D4**
Lake Station 14,294 **A3**
La Porte 21,796 **A4**
Lawrence 25,591 **E5**
Lebanon 11,456 **D5**
Logansport 17,731 **C5**
Madison 12,472 **G7**
Marion 35,874 **C6**
Martinsville 11,311 **F5**
Merrillville 27,677 **B3**
Michigan City
36,850 **A4**
Mishawaka 40,201 **A5**
Mount Vernon 7,656 **I2**
Muncie 77,216 **D7**
Munster 20,671 **A2**
New Albany 37,103 **H6**
New Castle 20,056 **E7**
Noblesville 12,056 **D6**
Peru 13,764 **C5**
Plymouth 7,693 **B5**
Portage 27,409 **A3**
Princeton 8,976 **H2**
Richmond 41,349 **E8**
Rockville 2,785 **E3**
Schererville 13,209 **B3**
Seymour 15,050 **G6**
Shelbyville 14,989 **F6**
South Bend 109,727 **A5**
Speedway 12,641 **E5**
Tell City 8,704 **I4**
Terre Haute 61,125 **F3**
Valparaiso 22,247 **B3**
Vincennes 20,857 **G2**
Wabash 12,985 **C6**
Warsaw 10,647 **B6**
Washington 11,325 **G3**
West Lafayette
21,247 **D4**

Statute Miles
5 0 5 10 15 20 25 30

Kilometers
5 0 5 15 25 35

A-520515-71 -7-8-10
COSMO SERIES INDIANA
Copyright by
RAND McNALLY & COMPANY
Made in U.S.A.

Lambert Conformal Conic Projection
SCALE 1:1,465,000 1 Inch = 23 Statute Miles

Indiana

POPULATION 5,570,800.
Rank: 14.*Density:* 155 people/mi²
(60 people/km²).*Urban:*
64.2%.*Rural:* 35.8%.
INCOME/CAPITA $11,780.
Rank: 30.
ENTERED UNION Dec. 11, 1816,
19th state.

CAPITAL Indianapolis, 727,500.
LARGEST CITY Indianapolis.
AREA 35,936 mi² (93,074 km²).
Rank: 38.*Water area:* 481 mi²
(1,246 km²).
DIMENSIONS N–S 265 miles,
E–W 160 miles.

ELEVATIONS *Highest:* In Wayne
County, 1,257 ft (383 m).*Lowest:*
Along Ohio River, 320 ft (98 m).
CLIMATE Hot, humid summers;
cold winters; moderate rainfall.

Indiana Dunes National Lakeshore
preserves nearly fifteen thousand
acres of beautiful and unusual terrain along Lake Michigan. There are
a number of environments here, including sandy beaches, sand dunes
of varying shapes and sizes, verdant
valleys, and low, flat marshlands. The
lakeshore is all the more unusual
because of its location within the
almost solidly urban and industrial
area near Gary, Indiana. At least two
hundred species of birds use the
lakeshore as a resting, nesting, or
wintering area. The formation of the
dunes is a gradual, lengthy process.
After sand is carried ashore by lake
water and swept inland by wind, it
can be blocked by hardy vegetation.
Grasses, shrubs, and small trees provide cores around which small sand
cones form, and as more windswept
sand enlarges the cones, they
become sand dunes.

From the air, the Indiana landscape takes on the appearance of a quilt, a colorful patchwork of rectangular fields bordered by country roads and highways. This geometric design is a result of the rectangular survey system, established in 1785 to divide the land into regular townships, ranges, and sections for its orderly settlement. The pattern is typical of the Midwest, where generations have followed the basic rectangular grid to scribe property with neat, straight boundaries and well-organized counties. The pattern holds true right down to the state's county seats. Platted around courthouses set in town squares, these local-government sites are connected to one another by an intricate, systematic network of state roads.

The state's agriculture, industry, and cultural life also reflect a quilt-like design, although the pattern is more often one of striking contrasts. Indiana is an industrial state that sustains a productive agricultural economy; an urban state with deep rural roots; and a tolerant state that has its share of racial divisions and tensions. Few states can point to an awesome battery of blast furnaces in one region and a collection of rustic covered bridges in another. The geographic and cultural patterns in Indiana reflect the great variety of American life that is concentrated in this state. It can claim some identity with all four regions of the country: the South, by proximity to the Ohio River; the North, in its industrial production; the East, by path of settlement; and the West, in its outlook on resources and values.

In the past decade, however, the pattern of Indiana's life has been subjected to considerable strain. Economic development has led to increased air and water pollution, and the recent economic recession has resulted in a decline in heavy industry. Overall, however, Indiana continues to weave together the essential strands of American life in all its diversity and contrasts. Despite the strains, the fabric still holds strong.

Land Use Indiana's pattern of land use is typical of
much of the upper Midwest, where productive farmland
and beautiful landscapes are spotted liberally with cities
of substantial size and industrial potential. On Indiana's
Lake Michigan shore, parks enclosing fragile sand dunes
lie adjacent to areas of heavy industry, which can be
damaging to the parklands if precautions are not taken.

Farmland (cropland
and pastureland)

Farmland
and woodlots

Forests

Livestock grazing (areas
other than farmland)

Major urban areas

Major highways

National interstate

U.S.

© RAND MC NALLY & CO.

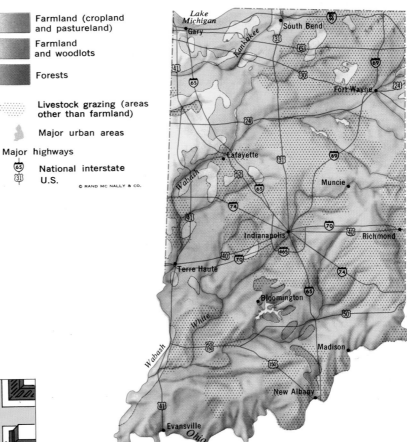

Town Settlement   The pattern of Indiana's settlement dates back to the horse-
and-buggy days, when much of daily life revolved around a centralized county
seat. The limited county size enabled taxpayers and other citizens to make the
round trip to the courthouse, and its surrounding facilities, within one day.

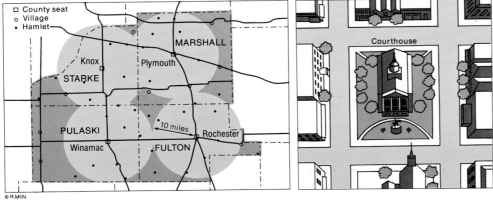

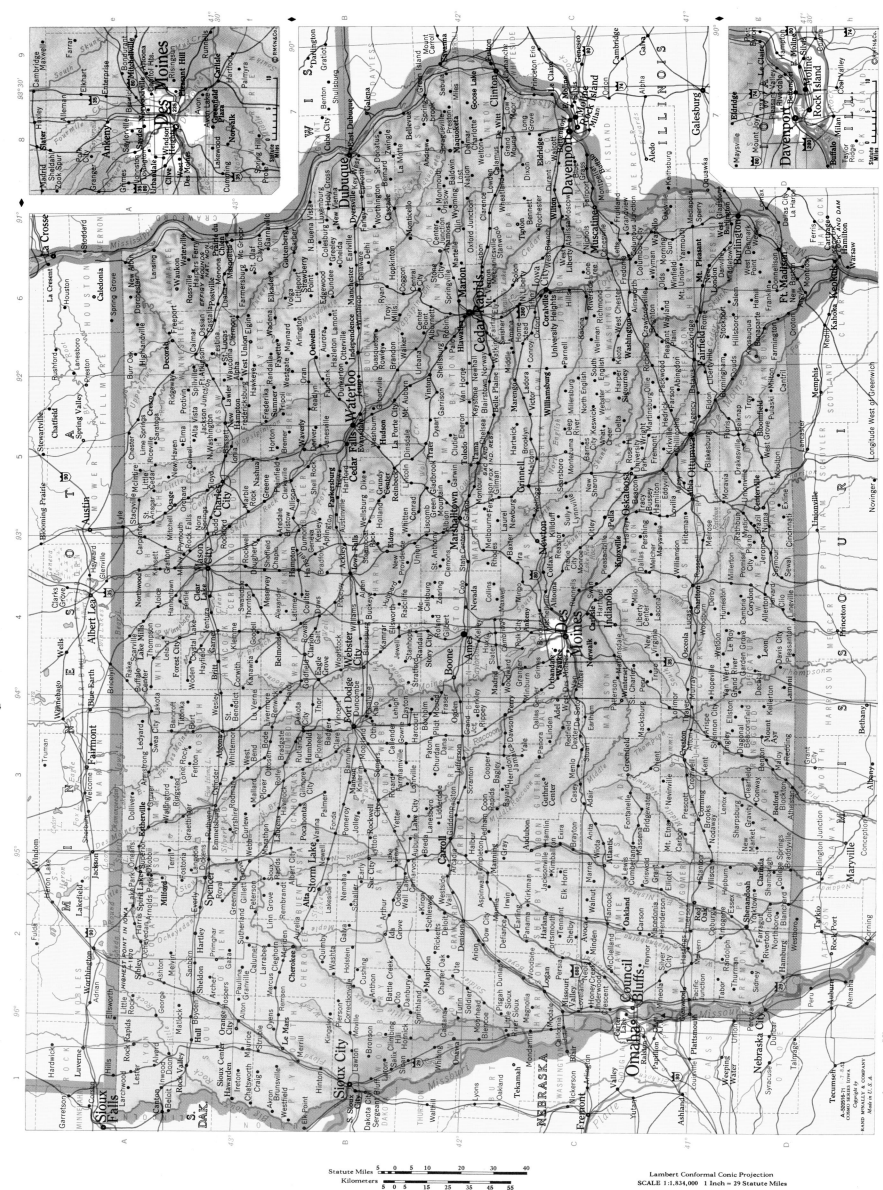

Cities and Towns

Algona 6,289 A3
Amana 600 C6
Ames 45,775 B4
Anamosa 4,958 B6
Ankeny 15,429 C4
Atlantic 7,789 C2
Bettendorf 27,381 C7
Boone 12,602 B4
Burlington 29,529 D6
Carroll 9,705 B3
Cedar Falls 36,322 B5
Cedar Rapids 110,243 C6
Centerville 6,558 D5
Chariton 4,987 C4
Charles City 8,778 A5
Cherokee 7,004 B2
Clarinda 5,458 D2
Clinton 32,828 C7
Council Bluffs 56,449 C2
Creston 8,429 C3
Davenport 103,264 C7
Decorah 7,991 A6
Denison 6,675 B2
Des Moines 191,003 C4
De Witt 4,512 C7
Dubuque 62,321 B7
Emmetsburg 4,621 A3
Estherville 7,518 A3
Fairfield 9,428 C6
Fort Dodge 29,423 B3
Fort Madison 13,520 D6
Glenwood 5,280 C2
Grinnell 8,868 C5
Guttenberg 2,428 B6
Hampton 4,630 B4
Harlan 5,357 C2
Humboldt 4,794 B3
Independence 6,392 B6
Indianola 10,843 C4
Iowa City 50,508 C6
Iowa Falls 6,174 B4
Jefferson 4,854 B3
Keokuk 13,536 D6
Knoxville 8,143 C4
Le Mars 8,276 B1
Manchester 4,942 B6
Maquoketa 6,313 B7
Marion 19,474 B6
Marshalltown 26,938 B5
Mason City 30,144 A4
Mount Pleasant 7,322 D6
Muscatine 23,467 C6
Newton 15,292 C4
Oelwein 7,564 B6
Orange City 4,588 B1
Oskaloosa 10,989 C5
Ottumwa 27,381 C5
Pella 8,349 C5
Perry 7,053 C3
Red Oak 6,810 D2
Sheldon 5,003 A2
Shenandoah 6,274 D2
Sioux Center 4,588 A1
Sioux City 82,003 B1
Spencer 11,726 A2
Storm Lake 8,814 B2
Urbandale 17,869 C4
Vinton 5,040 B5
Washington 6,584 C6
Waterloo 75,985 B5
Waverly 8,444 B5
Webster City 8,572 B4
West Branch 1,867 C6
West Des Moines 21,894 C4

Statute Miles 5 0 5 10 20 30 40
Kilometers 5 0 15 30 45 55

Lambert Conformal Conic Projection
SCALE 1:1,834,000 1 Inch = 29 Statute Miles

Iowa

POPULATION 2,860,700. *Rank:* 29.*Density:* 51 people/mi² (20 people/km²).*Urban:* 58.6%.*Rural:* 41.4%. **INCOME/CAPITA** $12,123. *Rank:* 26. **ENTERED UNION** Dec. 28, 1846, 29th state.	**CAPITAL** Des Moines, 194,100. **LARGEST CITY** Des Moines. **LAND AREA** 55,965 mi² (144,949 km²). *Rank:* 23.*Water area:* 310 mi² (803 km²). **DIMENSIONS** N–S 205 miles, E–W 310 miles.	**ELEVATIONS** *Highest:* In Osceola County, 1,670 ft (509 m).*Lowest:* Along Mississippi River, 480 ft (146 m). **CLIMATE** Hot summers with ample rainfall; cold winters with some heavy snows.

Iowa lies in the heart of the American Midwest, the most productive agricultural region in the world. This location has made the state an agricultural leader, producing the grains and livestock needed by the United States and world markets. But the state is also positioned on the fringe of Midwest industrialization, and its future may depend on its ability to balance farming with a diversified and changing industrial sector.

Even in the fertile Midwest, few states are blessed with as much prime tillable acreage or quite so abundant an agriculture. Nearly all of Iowa's soil is cultivable, and the state is a leader in soybean, corn, and livestock production. Ironically, this landlocked state makes a major contribution to America's foreign trade, selling grain to many other nations. However, this trade also makes Iowa vulnerable to foreign-policy decisions, including grain embargoes and taxes levied by governments at home and abroad.

Given Iowa's reputation as an agricultural producer, many people would be surprised that much of the state's income is derived from manufacturing. More Iowans live in cities than on farms, a situation common in other modern agricultural states. Iowa's total manufacturing output, however, is much below that of more heavily industrialized states, despite the industrial enclaves found in many of its cities. In addition, its mineral resources are negligible. But the remarkable homogeneity of Iowa's people may facilitate achievement of a unified consensus regarding the state's development and direction.

Iowa will need to diversify its economy even more in the future. Its agriculture is often caught between low market prices and the expense of machinery, fuel, fertilizers, and other supplies needed to maintain high agricultural production. As a result, Iowans are attempting to develop new industries and a better climate for business and at the same time trying to expand and stabilize markets for their agricultural products. They are hopeful that industry will provide as rich a yield as the land has given them.

Land Use Iowa is the model of an ideal farm state. Layers of fertile topsoil cover virtually the entire state; low relief—mostly flat prairies and rolling hills—makes the land easily tillable by humans and machines; water is available in just the right quantities; and the growing season is perfect for a variety of grain and feed crops. A system of cities evenly placed across the landscape connects farmers to sources of farm supplies and out-of-state markets.

- Farmland (cropland and pastureland)
- Farmland and woodlots
- Livestock grazing (areas other than farmland)
- Major urban areas

Major highways
- 80 National interstate
- 61 U.S.

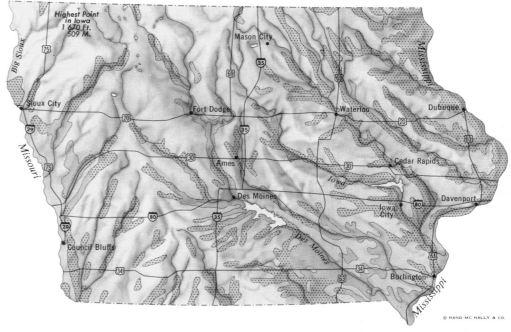

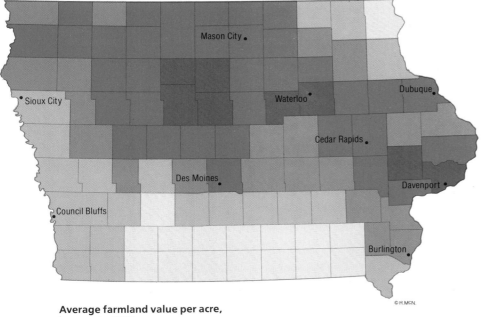

Average farmland value per acre, by county, 1982

- $2,400 or more
- $2,000–$2,400
- $1,600–$2,000
- $1,200–$1,600
- $800–$1,200

Land Value Some of the best farmland in the world is found in Iowa; and soybeans and corn mean well-being for the farmers of the state. The amount of soybeans and corn that an area can produce determines the value of the land, and natural and human factors combine to influence productivity. Nature provides level terrain, good soils, and adequate heat and moisture, and by tiling for drainage and terracing to prevent erosion, farmers increase the amount of land on which these cash crops can be grown.

Iowa's population is more urban than rural, its economy is diversifying into areas other than agriculture, and large, mechanized farms are eliminating the small family farms of the past. Yet even with all these changes, much of Iowa's strength still lies in the small towns that dot the countryside. Eldorado, in the northeastern section of the state, has a population just over one hundred and symbolizes the picturesque American small town that is partly responsible for Iowa's reputation as the typical midwestern state.

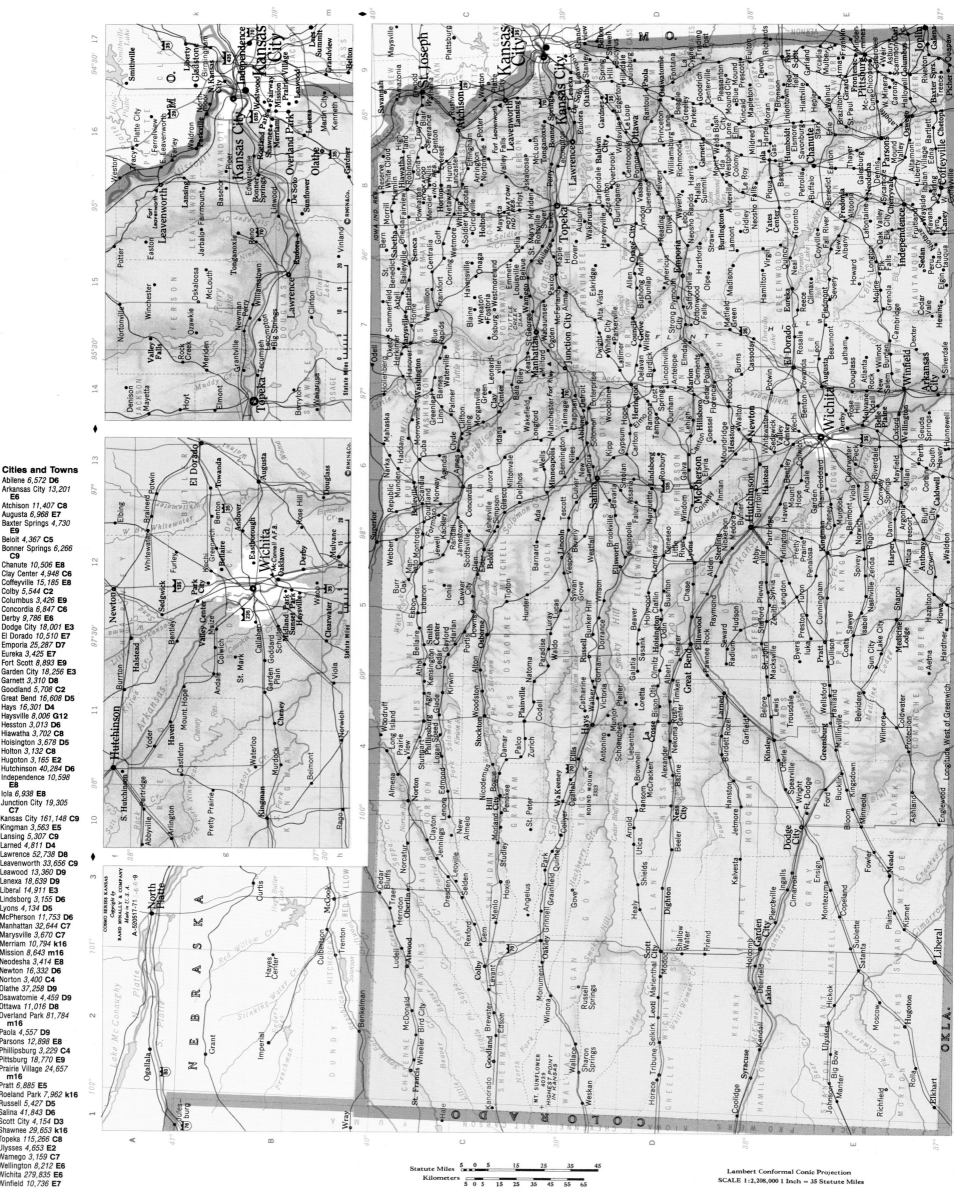

Cities and Towns

Abilene 6,572 D6
Arkansas City 13,201 E6
Atchison 11,407 C8
Augusta 6,968 E7
Baxter Springs 4,730 E9
Beloit 4,367 C5
Bonner Springs 6,266 C9
Chanute 10,506 E8
Clay Center 4,948 C6
Coffeyville 15,185 E8
Colby 5,544 C2
Columbus 3,426 E9
Concordia 6,847 C6
Derby 9,786 E6
Dodge City 18,001 E3
El Dorado 10,510 E7
Emporia 25,287 D7
Eureka 3,425 E7
Fort Scott 8,893 E9
Garden City 18,256 E3
Garnett 3,310 D8
Goodland 5,708 C2
Great Bend 16,608 D5
Hays 16,301 D4
Haysville 8,006 G12
Hesston 3,013 D6
Hiawatha 3,702 C8
Hoisington 3,678 D5
Holton 3,132 C8
Hugoton 3,165 E2
Hutchinson 40,284 D6
Independence 10,598 E8
Iola 6,938 E8
Junction City 19,305 C7
Kansas City 161,148 C9
Kingman 3,563 E5
Lansing 5,307 C9
Larned 4,811 D4
Lawrence 52,738 D8
Leavenworth 33,656 C9
Leawood 13,360 D9
Lenexa 18,639 D9
Liberal 14,911 E3
Lindsborg 3,155 D6
Lyons 4,134 D5
McPherson 11,753 D6
Manhattan 32,644 C7
Marysville 3,670 C7
Merriam 10,794 k16
Mission 8,643 m16
Neodesha 3,414 E8
Newton 16,332 D6
Norton 3,400 C4
Olathe 37,258 D9
Osawatomie 4,459 D9
Ottawa 11,016 D8
Overland Park 81,784 m16
Paola 4,557 D9
Parsons 12,898 E8
Phillipsburg 3,229 C4
Pittsburg 18,770 E9
Prairie Village 24,657 m16
Pratt 6,885 E5
Roeland Park 7,962 k16
Russell 5,427 D5
Salina 41,843 D6
Scott City 4,154 D3
Shawnee 29,653 k16
Topeka 115,266 C8
Ulysses 4,653 E2
Wamego 3,159 C7
Wellington 8,212 E6
Wichita 279,835 E6
Winfield 10,736 E7

Statute Miles

Kilometers

COSMO SERIES KANSAS
Copyright by
RAND McNALLY & COMPANY
Made in U.S.A.
A-520517-71 -6-6-9

Lambert Conformal Conic Projection
SCALE 1:2,208,000 1 Inch = 35 Statute Miles

Kansas

POPULATION   2,495,000.
Rank: 32.*Density:* 31 people/mi²
(12 people/km²).*Urban:*
66.7%.*Rural:* 33.3%.
INCOME/CAPITA $13,367.
Rank: 16.
ENTERED UNION   Jan. 29, 1861,
34th state.

CAPITAL   Topeka, 122,000.
LARGEST CITY   Wichita, 292,700.
LAND AREA   81,783 mi²
(211,817 km²).
Rank: 13.*Water area:* 499 mi²
(1,292 km²).
DIMENSIONS   N–S 205 miles,
E–W 410 miles.

ELEVATIONS   *Highest:* Mount
Sunflower, 4,039 ft
(1,231 m).*Lowest:* Along Verdigris
River,
680 ft (207 m).
CLIMATE   Cold winters, hot
summers; moderate rainfall in
east, diminishing in west.

Kansas often presents an image at odds with its reality. For decades the state was simply a stopover on the trail leading to more glamorous frontiers in the Oregon Territory and California goldfields. Even the incentive for settling the state arose not from the land itself but from the nation's growing conflict over the spread of slavery. Both the North and the South wanted this strategic territory as an ally. Despite its dubious beginnings, Kansas has emerged as a productive and progressive member of the nation.

Early settlement of the region was slow because most pioneers considered it desert land. Used to the rich, dark soils of the East, they believed Kansas's endless prairies were too dry for farming. Then in the 1870's, Mennonite settlers brought a hardy variety of Eastern European wheat, which flourished in the productive soil of the plains. Today, Kansas is one of the greatest grain-producing regions in the world.

Yet even this image belies reality. The present income of Kansas is based on industry as well as agriculture, and the state manufactures a variety of goods, including aircraft, camping gear, air-conditioning equipment, and snowmobiles. Kansas benefits as well from its strong standing as a mineral producer, exporting oil, coal, cement, lead, zinc, salt, and stone.

It would also be a mistake to equate Kansas's position at the geographic center of the United States with middle-of-the-road conservatism in its cultural and political life. Actually, Kansas has a progressive and innovative history that includes the Populist Party, direct primaries, women's suffrage, and public assistance for the needy. In the 1950's, the first court case declaring segregation in public schools as unconstitutional served as a precedent for other decisions regarding civil rights in school systems.

With its productive land, prospering industries, and forward-looking population, Kansas continues to play an important role in American life. From its central location, the state not only provides material wealth but also sets an example for the rest of the nation to follow.

Kansas is a major wheat producer, primarily in its western and central sections. As is true throughout the nation, extensive mechanization of farms has changed the economic structure of farming. The increase in fixed costs for machines means more land is needed per farm to make a profit. Also, with the present use of modern self-propelled combines, harvesting can be accomplished with a comparatively small number of workers. The increase in farm size and the decrease in farm population are nationwide trends, and although relatively stabilized, they are expected to continue.

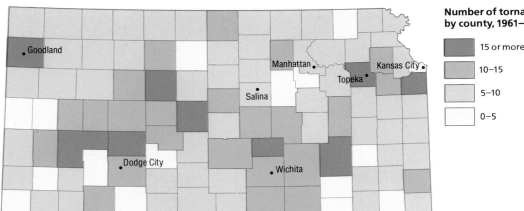

Number of tornadoes, by county, 1961–1981

- 15 or more
- 10–15
- 5–10
- 0–5

Tornadoes   The meeting of air masses that have contrasting characteristics of temperature, moisture, density, and airflow tends to trigger many tornadoes in Kansas, Oklahoma, and Texas. Kansas records a high percentage of these disturbances, but loss of life is decreasing because of better understanding and prediction of their occurrence.

Land Use   Millions of years ago, most of Kansas's land lay at the bottom of a large inland sea, and the good soil that remained after these waters drained away was supplemented through glacial activity. These processes left Kansas with many fertile prairies of low, rolling relief—ideal for agriculture. The northeastern region has the most productive land, while lack of rain and a higher sand content leaves the southwestern corner of the state with slightly lower productivity. Severe droughts in the 1930's and 1950's brought to the state's attention the importance of conserving soil and water. Today, water is held in artificial lakes and ponds, where it cannot wash away soil, and eventually it is released to nourish crops. Farmers now use contour plowing, terracing and shelterbelts of trees to conserve soil and water and to protect fields from wind erosion.

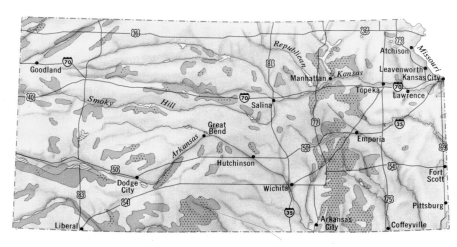

- Farmland (cropland and pastureland)
- Farmland and woodlots
- Forests
- Grassland
- Irrigated areas
- Livestock grazing (areas other than farmland)
- Major urban areas

Major highways
- National interstate
- U.S.

© RAND McNALLY & CO.

Cities and Towns

Adrian 21,186 G6
Albion 11,059 F6
Alpena 12,214 C7
Ann Arbor 107,966 F7
Battle Creek 35,724 F5
Bay City 41,593 E7
Benton Harbor 14,707 F4
Big Rapids 14,361 E5
Birmingham 21,689 F7
Burton 29,976 F7
Cadillac 10,199 D5
Cheboygan 5,106 C6
Coldwater 9,461 G5
Dearborn 90,660 F7
Dearborn Heights 67,706 p15
Detroit 1,203,339 F7
East Detroit 38,280 p16
East Lansing 51,392 F6
Escanaba 14,355 C3
Farmington Hills 58,056 o15
Flint 159,611 E7
Garden City 35,640 p15
Grand Haven 11,763 E4
Grand Rapids 181,843 F5
Grosse Pointe Woods 18,886 p16
Hamtramck 12,300 p15
Highland Park 27,909 p15
Holland 26,281 F4
Houghton 7,512 A2
Iron Mountain 8,341 C2
Ironwood 7,741 n11
Jackson 39,739 F6
Kalamazoo 79,722 F5
Kentwood 30,438 F5
Lansing 130,414 F6
Lincoln Park 45,105 p15
Livonia 104,814 F7
Ludington 8,937 E4
Mackinaw City 820 C6
Madison Heights 35,375 o15
Manistee 7,566 D4
Marquette 23,288 B3
Menominee 10,099 C3
Midland 37,250 E6
Monroe 23,531 G7
Mount Pleasant 23,746 E6
Muskegon 40,823 E4
Niles 13,115 G4
Norton Shores 22,025 E4
Novi 22,525 p15
Oak Park 31,537 p15
Owosso 16,455 E6
Petoskey 6,097 C6
Pontiac 76,715 F7
Portage 38,157 F5
Port Huron 33,981 F8
Romulus 24,857 p15
Roseville 54,311 o16
Royal Oak 70,893 F7
Saginaw 77,508 E7
St. Clair Shores 76,210 p16
Sault Ste. Marie 14,448 B6
Southfield 75,568 o15
Southgate 32,058 p15
Sterling Heights 108,999 o15
Sturgis 9,468 G5
Taylor 77,568 p15
Traverse City 15,516 D5
Trenton 22,762 F7
Troy 67,102 o15
Warren 161,134 F7
Westland 84,603 F7
Wyandotte 34,006 F7
Wyoming 59,616 F5
Ypsilanti 24,031 F7

Statute Miles 5 0 5 10 20 30 40 50
Kilometers 5 0 5 15 30 45 60 75

Lambert Conformal Conic Projection
SCALE 1:2,347,000 1 Inch = 37 Statute Miles

Michigan

POPULATION 9,262,900.
Rank: 8.*Density:* 163 people/mi² (63 people/km²).*Urban:* 70.7%.*Rural:* 29.3%.
INCOME/CAPITA $12,751.
Rank: 21.
ENTERED UNION Jan. 26, 1837, 26th state.

CAPITAL Lansing, 130,700.
LARGEST CITY Detroit, 1,082,200.
LAND AREA 56,959 mi² (147,523 km²).
Rank: 22.*Water area:* 40,148 mi² (103,983 km²)
DIMENSIONS N–S 400 miles, E–W 310 miles.

ELEVATIONS *Highest:* Mount Curwood, 1,980 ft (604 m).*Lowest:* Lake Erie shoreline, 572 ft (174 m).
CLIMATE Cold, snowy winters; mild summers; adequate rainfall.

Michigan's role in the Midwest has largely been determined by the Great Lakes, which divide the state into a lower and an upper peninsula. The Lower Peninsula, larger and more populated, is the home of heavy industry. Though Detroit has long been recognized as the automobile capital of the world, manufacturing is spread throughout the peninsula, in such cities as Flint, Lansing, Grand Rapids, and Muskegon. The Upper Peninsula is primarily wilderness, rich in copper, iron ores, and heavy stands of timber. Tourism is important to both regions, with their dense forests, glacial lakes, and great stretches of beach along Lake Michigan and Lake Huron.

Low-cost water transport on the Great Lakes was a key factor in encouraging the concentration of manufacturing in Michigan. Raw materials and finished products could be shipped easily and cheaply into and out of the state. Along the coastal zone, the lakes also affect the weather, moderating winter and summer temperatures, and thus are vital to the state's agriculture. Slight differences in temperature can mean success or failure for the state's fruit and vegetable crops.

Michigan faces the last decades of the twentieth century with a number of difficult problems. The manufacturing that made the state one of the pivotal areas in the nation's economy is now suffering under the double assault of an overall decline of heavy industry and a rise in foreign competition in the automobile and steel industries. Further, although mineral and timber resources continue to provide jobs and revenue, these resources have been seriously depleted by well over a century of industrial use. High unemployment, urban redevelopment, and technological change are issues that will occupy a prominent place on Michigan's future agenda.

There are no easy solutions, but Michigan has weathered economic storms before. And although experiencing the turmoil of change sweeping the country, at a deeper level, Michigan may harbor an enduring strength that will enable it to keep stride with national trends.

Land Use Michigan has abundant plant and animal life, primarily because of its mild summer weather and moderate, evenly distributed rainfall. The Great Lakes increase humidity, lessen frosts, and prolong growing seasons in the state. Southern Michigan's rich, sandy soils are especially suited for agriculture.

Centrally located on the Great Lakes—St. Lawrence Seaway system, Detroit is one of the nation's busiest ports. Ships deliver raw materials for use in the city's factories and pick up automobiles, automobile parts, and other products for shipment to United States and foreign markets. Supplementing Detroit's water transportation is a network of rail, air, and truck routes, all of which have contributed to the development of Detroit's industry. But because of the city's dependence on commerce and industries such as automaking, it is also dependent upon market forces outside of its control. Thus, Detroit often acts as a barometer of the national economy, being one of the first areas to register a decline or rise in employment and profits.

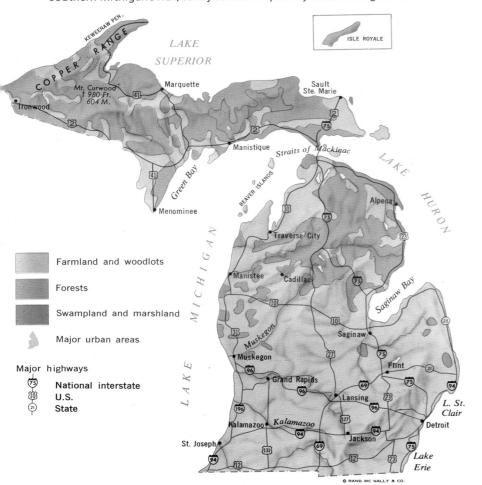

Farmland and woodlots

Forests

Swampland and marshland

Major urban areas

Major highways

75 National interstate

10 U.S.

21 State

The Great Lakes The Great Lakes and St. Lawrence River form one of the most important inland waterway systems in the world, linking the cities of the United States interior with the Atlantic Ocean. With coasts bordering all but Lake Ontario, Michigan was shaped by and profits from its key position on this international transportation artery. The lakes provide access not only to international shipping routes, but also to abundant quantities of water and an incomparable recreational resource.

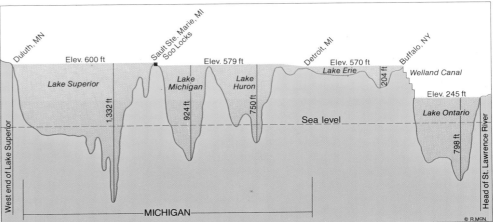

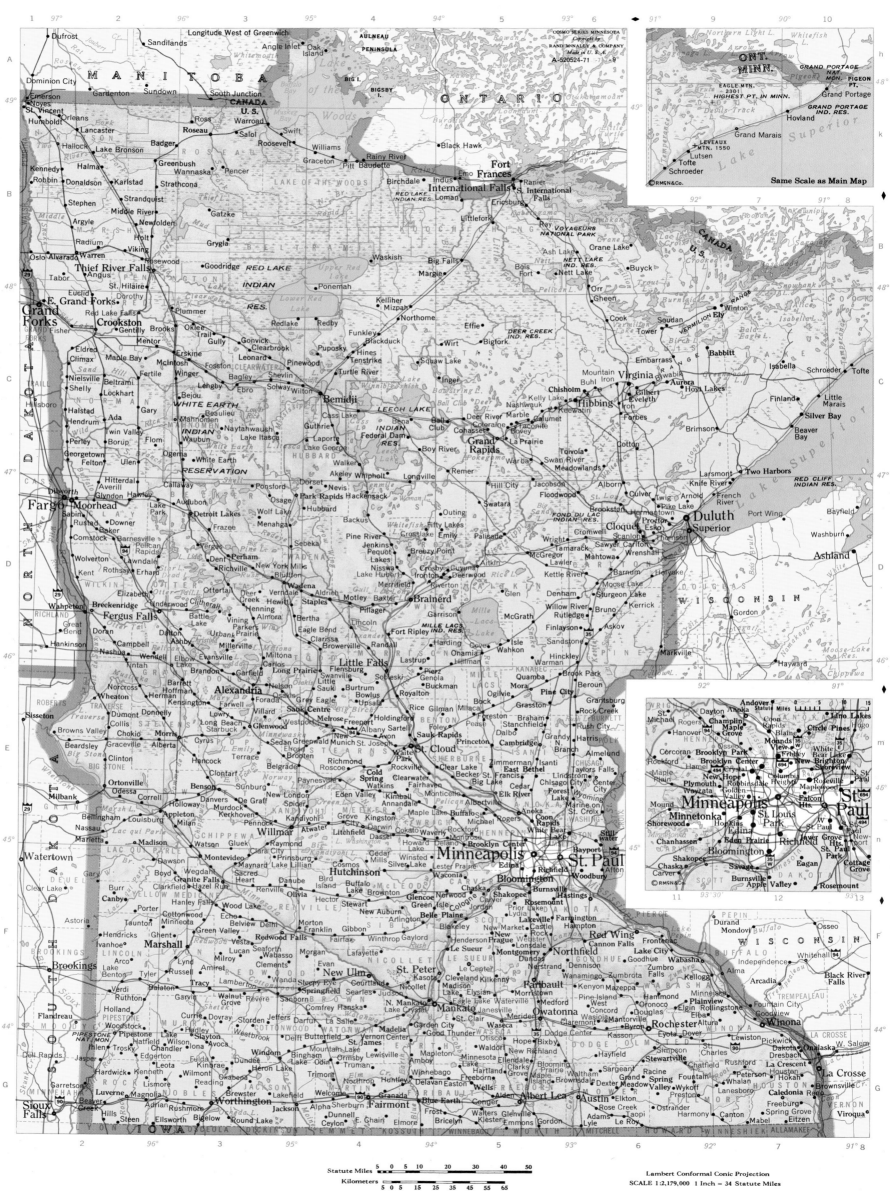

Cities and Towns

Albert Lea 19,200 **G5**
Alexandria 7,608 **E3**
Anoka 15,634 **E5**
Apple Valley 21,818 **n12**
Austin 23,020 **G6**
Bemidji 10,949 **C4**
Blaine 28,558 **m12**
Bloomington 81,831 **F5**
Brainerd 11,489 **D4**
Brooklyn Center 31,230 **E5**
Brooklyn Park 43,332 **m12**
Burnsville 35,674 **F5**
Chisholm 5,930 **C6**
Cloquet 11,142 **D6**
Columbia Heights 20,029 **m12**
Coon Rapids 35,826 **E5**
Cottage Grove 18,994 **n13**
Crookston 8,628 **C2**
Crystal 25,543 **m12**
Detroit Lakes 7,106 **D3**
Duluth 92,811 **D6**
Eagan 20,700 **n12**
East Bethel 6,626 **E5**
East Grand Forks 8,537 **C2**
Eden Prairie 16,263 **n12**
Edina 46,073 **F5**
Ely 4,820 **C7**
Fairmont 11,506 **G4**
Faribault 16,241 **F5**
Fergus Falls 12,519 **D2**
Fridley 30,228 **m12**
Golden Valley 22,775 **n12**
Grand Marais 1,289 **k9**
Grand Rapids 7,934 **C5**
Hibbing 21,193 **C6**
Hutchinson 9,244 **F4**
International Falls 5,611 **B5**
Inver Grove Heights 17,171 **n12**
Lakeville 14,790 **F5**
Litchfield 5,904 **E4**
Little Falls 7,250 **E4**
Mankato 28,651 **F5**
Maple Grove 20,525 **m12**
Maplewood 26,990 **n12**
Marshall 11,161 **F3**
Minneapolis 370,951 **F5**
Minnetonka 38,683 **n12**
Montevideo 5,845 **F3**
Moorhead 29,998 **D2**
Morris 5,367 **E3**
New Brighton 23,269 **m12**
New Hope 23,087 **m12**
New Ulm 13,755 **F4**
Northfield 12,562 **F5**
Owatonna 18,632 **F5**
Pipestone 4,887 **G2**
Plymouth 31,615 **m12**
Red Wing 13,736 **F6**
Redwood Falls 5,210 **F3**
Richfield 37,851 **F5**
Rochester 57,890 **F6**
Roseville 35,820 **m12**
St. Cloud 42,566 **E4**
St. Louis Park 42,931 **F5**
St. Paul 270,230 **F5**
St. Peter 9,056 **F5**
Shoreview 17,300 **m12**
South St. Paul 21,235 **n12**
Thief River Falls 9,105 **B2**
Virginia 11,056 **C6**
Waseca 8,219 **F5**
West St. Paul 18,527 **n12**
White Bear Lake 22,538 **E5**
Willmar 15,895 **E3**
Winona 25,075 **F7**
Worthington 10,243 **G3**

Minnesota

POPULATION 4,292,300.
Rank: 21.*Density:* 54 people/mi²
(21 people/km²).*Urban:*
66.9%.*Rural:* 33.1%.
INCOME/CAPITA $13,607.
Rank: 11.
ENTERED UNION May 11, 1858,
32nd state.

CAPITAL St. Paul, 274,700.
LARGEST CITY Minneapolis,
370,200.
LAND AREA 79,548 mi²
(206,028 km²).
Rank: 14.*Water area:* 7,066 mi²
(18,301 km²)
DIMENSIONS N–S 400 miles,
E–W 350 miles.

ELEVATIONS *Highest:* Eagle
Mountain, 2,301 ft
(701 m).*Lowest:* Lake Superior
shoreline, 602 ft (183 m).
CLIMATE Long, cold winters; short
summers; moderate rainfall.

While immense glaciers shaped the landscape and character of Minnesota millions of years ago, its people have created a rich, productive life in this varied and surprising land. Although many states bear marks of the Ice Age, almost all of the features for which Minnesota is best known—its iron ore, myriad blue lakes, and fertile southern farmland—reflect glacial action.

In the northern part of the state, retreating ice exposed the iron-rich bedrock of the Canadian Shield, making Minnesota a major source of high-quality ore for the American steel industry. The Mesabi iron-ore range in the northwest was once one of the world's greatest mining regions. Although producing lower-quality ore today, the range is still an important supplier.

As the great glaciers melted, they left behind new soil, rock deposits, and waterways. Streams and lakes by the thousands were created, giving Minnesota one of the greatest water areas of all the states and a reputation as a wonderland for outdoor recreation. Dairy and feed-grain farms place Minnesota in the company of its neighbors, who form the great agricultural heartland of the nation.

It is Minnesota's people, however, who put these resources to work. Settled first by New Englanders, the state quickly became the adopted home of hardworking Swedish, German, and Norwegian families. Within a few decades, Minneapolis and St. Paul were the dominant centers of the upper Midwest, extending their influence from western Wisconsin to Montana and south to Iowa. From the late nineteenth to the early twentieth centuries, Minnesota was a leading exporter of flour, lumber, and iron ore.

Today, Minnesota must adapt to an economy less dependent on these primary products. The iron ranges in the north and the agricultural lands in the south are losing population as demand for Minnesota's products declines and as farming becomes more mechanized. But overall, the state has adjusted remarkably well to change, and Minnesota continues to play an important part in the economy of the upper Midwest region. Its natural beauty and the quality of life fashioned by its population attract people and businesses each year.

Positioned at the end of the Great Lakes–St. Lawrence Seaway system, Duluth acts as the commercial center of northern Minnesota. This port provides access to markets for agricultural and industrial goods produced both inside and outside the state, including iron ore from Minnesota's ranges and grain from the fields of North and South Dakota.

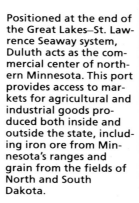

Glacial Effects The history of Minnesota can be traced in the lakes, streams, and landforms created millions of years ago by the glaciers. In the north, the glaciers' scouring action exposed the iron-rich deposits of the Mesabi Range. Agricultural lands were provided by deposits left on the outwash plains. And the kettle lakes, esker troughs, and other depressions established the state's topography in its lake, stream, and forest regions, the focal points of a successful tourist industry.

Till plain
Moraine
Outwash
Lake plain
Bedrock

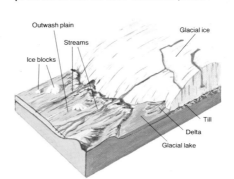

Land Use Minnesota lies across an important continental divide between midwestern prairies and northern forests, and this division is apparent in the state's land use. Farming is concentrated in the south, where prairie soils support a productive agriculture. Marking the limit of America's prairies, northern forests contribute to the state's wood-products industry.

Farmland (cropland and pastureland)

Farmland and woodlots

Forests

Swampland and marshland

Major urban areas

Major highways

National interstate
U.S.

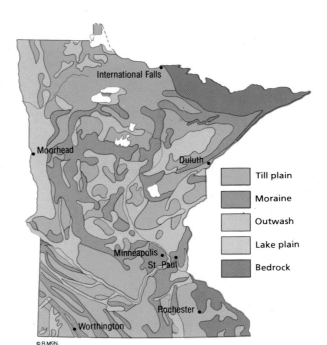

Retreating Glacier The body and meltwater of a glacier carry and deposit a variety of materials—including clay, sand, gravel, and boulders—which comprise both the till and outwash plains.

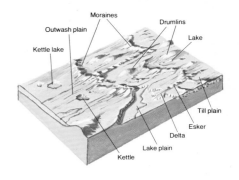

After a glacial mass has retreated from an area, the many new landforms that have been created under its surface and from its meltwater are exposed to view.

Cities and Towns

Arnold 19,141 **C7**
Aurora 6,437 **E4**
Ballwin 12,656 **f12**
Belton 12,708 **C3**
Berkeley 15,922 **f13**
Blue Springs 25,927 **h11**
Bolivar 5,919 **D4**
Boonville 6,959 **C5**
Branson 2,550 **E4**
Bridgeton 18,445 **C7**
Cape Girardeau 34,361 **D8**
Carthage 11,104 **D3**
Caruthersville 7,958 **E8**
Charleston 5,230 **E8**
Chillicothe 9,089 **B4**
Clayton 14,273 **f13**
Clinton 8,366 **C4**
Columbia 62,061 **C5**
Concord 20,896 **f13**
De Soto 5,993 **C7**
Dexter 7,043 **E8**
Eureka 3,862 **f12**
Excelsior Springs 10,424 **B3**
Farmington 8,270 **D7**
Ferguson 24,740 **C7**
Festus 7,574 **C7**
Florissant 55,372 **f13**
Fulton 10,145 **C6**
Gladstone 24,990 **h10**
Grandview 24,502 **C3**
Hannibal 18,811 **B6**
Independence 111,806 **B3**
Jackson 7,827 **D8**
Jefferson City 33,619 **C5**
Jennings 17,026 **f13**
Joplin 39,023 **D3**
Kansas City 448,159 **B3**
Kennett 10,145 **E7**
Kirksville 17,167 **A5**
Kirkwood 27,987 **f13**
Lebanon 9,507 **D5**
Lees Summit 28,741 **C3**
Liberty 16,251 **B3**
Malden 6,096 **E8**
Marshall 12,781 **B4**
Maryville 9,558 **A3**
Mehlville 22,900 **f13**
Mexico 12,276 **B6**
Moberly 13,418 **B5**
Monett 6,148 **E4**
Neosho 9,493 **E3**
Nevada 9,044 **D3**
Overland 19,620 **f13**
Perryville 7,343 **D8**
Poplar Bluff 17,139 **E7**
Raytown 31,759 **h11**
Richmond Heights 11,516 **f13**
Rolla 13,303 **D6**
St. Charles 37,379 **C7**
Ste. Genevieve 4,481 **D7**
St. Joseph 76,691 **B3**
St. Louis 453,085 **C7**
St. Peters 14,700 **C7**
Sappington 11,388 **f13**
Sedalia 20,927 **C4**
Sikeston 17,431 **E8**
Spanish Lake 20,632 **f13**
Springfield 133,116 **D4**
Sullivan 5,461 **C6**
Trenton 6,811 **A4**
University City 42,738 **C7**
Warrensburg 13,807 **C4**
Washington 9,251 **C6**
Webster Groves 23,097 **f13**
West Plains 7,741 **E6**

Statute Miles 5 0 5 15 25 35 45
Kilometers 5 0 5 15 25 35 45 55 65

Lambert Conformal Conic Projection
SCALE 1:2,283,000   1 Inch = 36 Statute Miles

Missouri

POPULATION 5,173,600.
Rank: 15.*Density:* 75 people/mi²
(29 people/km²).*Urban:*
68.1%.*Rural:* 31.9%.
INCOME/CAPITA $12,202.
Rank: 25.
ENTERED UNION Aug. 10, 1821,
24th state.

CAPITAL Jefferson City, 36,700.
LARGEST CITY Kansas City,
446,100.
LAND AREA 68,945 mi²
(178,567 km²).
Rank: 18.*Water area:* 752 mi²
(1,948 km²).
DIMENSIONS N–S 280 miles,
E–W 300 miles.

ELEVATIONS *Highest:* Taum Sauk
Mountain, 1,772 ft
(540 m).*Lowest:* Along St. Francis
River, 230 ft (70 m).
CLIMATE Generally hot summers,
cold winters; moderate rainfall.

Missouri stands at a crossroads among the states. Here the forested areas of the East meet the plains of the West, and the cornfields of the North border the cotton fields of the South. The state is also a transportation center, linking the East, West, North, and South with air, rail, water, and truck routes.

Missouri has a long history as the Gateway to America's West, a reputation commemorated in the monumental Gateway Arch in St. Louis. Both the Santa Fe and Oregon trails originated in the state, and so many pioneers traveled through Missouri on their way West that it wasn't long before the state itself was settled. Its rich prairies and grasslands supported a variety of grain and seed crops, and the state quickly found its niche as an important grain and cattle market.

Missouri's key position at the head of supply routes to the western regions encouraged the development of manufacturing as well. The Missouri and Mississippi rivers converge near St. Louis, and the city once marked the northernmost limit of navigation for oceangoing vessels traveling up the Mississippi. In addition, decades of competition between the commercial centers of St. Louis and Chicago spurred the growth of commerce and industry in the state.

Today, Missouri is a leader in the production of aerospace and transportation equipment, including cars, trucks, and trains. Furthermore, Missouri makes a contribution to the country's mineral production. And it is a mark of the state's continued importance in midwestern and western finance that it is the site of two of the country's twelve Federal Reserve banks.

But Missouri's crossroads position creates problems as well as opportunities. For decades, rural people from the South have been migrating to urban areas, and the state's urban populace is now suffering from the industrial decline affecting many of the country's cities. Recent developments in service and professional industries and urban-renewal projects may be essential first steps in solving current problems and preparing for the future. Missouri today may stand at the crossroads of a movement toward a new economy and a new way of life.

The Ozark National Scenic Riverways contain miles of free-flowing streams. Natural underground water reservoirs feed the area's many springs, which in turn feed the rivers. Shown here is the Alley Springs flow on the Jacks Fork River.

Land Use In Missouri, pioneers found prime land for farming and industry. To the north and west are plains that are capable of supporting a productive agriculture and that are similar to land found in Iowa, Nebraska, and Kansas. The southeastern corner of the state lies in the Mississippi River's alluvial basin, which the state shares with its southern neighbors. Finally, the Ozark Plateau covers much of the state south of the Missouri River and is reminiscent of the forested uplands east of the Mississippi.

Farmland (cropland and pastureland)

Farmland and woodlots

Forests

Livestock grazing (areas other than farmland)

Major urban areas

Major highways

44 National interstate

66 U.S.

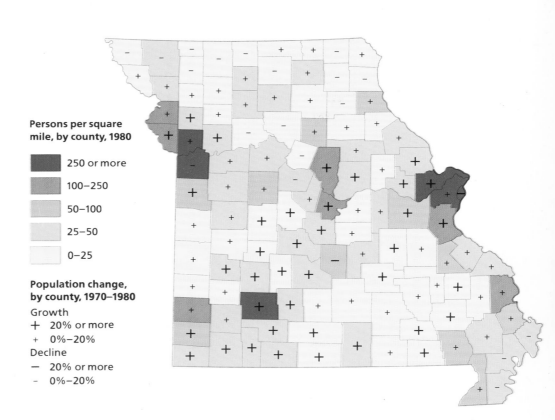

Persons per square mile, by county, 1980

250 or more

100–250

50–100

25–50

0–25

Population change, by county, 1970–1980

Growth
+ 20% or more
+ 0%–20%
Decline
− 20% or more
− 0%–20%

Population Change Missouri's North-South crossroads position is reflected in its population change of the past decade. In the northern United States, many rural areas have been faced with decreasing population, and northern Missouri seems to ally with this region in its pattern of population loss. In the southern part of the country, population growth is often the rule, and southern Missouri displays this general trend.

Cities and Towns

Ainsworth 2,256 **B6**
Albion 1,997 **C7**
Alliance 9,920 **B3**
Ashland 2,274 **C9**
Atkinson 1,521 **B7**
Auburn 3,482 **D10**
Aurora 3,717 **D7**
Beatrice 12,891 **D9**
Bellevue 21,813 **C10**
Blair 6,418 **C9**
Bridgeport 1,668 **C2**
Broken Bow 3,979 **C6**
Central City 3,083 **C7**
Chadron 5,933 **B3**
Columbus 17,328 **C8**
Cozad 4,453 **D6**
Crete 4,872 **D9**
David City 2,514 **C8**
Fairbury 4,885 **D8**
Falls City 5,374 **D10**
Fremont 23,979 **C9**
Fullerton 1,506 **C8**
Geneva 2,400 **D8**
Gering 7,760 **C2**
Gibbon 1,531 **D7**
Gordon 2,167 **B3**
Gothenburg 3,479 **D5**
Grand Island 33,180 **D7**
Gretna 1,609 **C9**
Hartington 1,730 **B8**
Hastings 23,045 **D7**
Hebron 1,906 **D8**
Holdrege 5,624 **D6**
Imperial 1,941 **D4**
Kearney 21,158 **D6**
Kimball 3,120 **C2**
La Vista 9,588 **g12**
Lexington 7,040 **D6**
Lincoln 171,932 **D9**
McCook 8,404 **D5**
Madison 1,950 **C8**
Milford 2,108 **D8**
Minden 2,939 **D7**
Mitchell 1,956 **C2**
Nebraska City 7,127 **D10**
Neligh 1,893 **B7**
Norfolk 19,449 **B8**
North Platte 24,509 **C5**
Ogallala 5,638 **C4**
Omaha 313,911 **C10**
O'Neill 4,049 **B7**
Ord 2,658 **C7**
Papillion 6,399 **C9**
Pierce 1,535 **B8**
Plattsmouth 6,295 **D10**
Ralston 5,143 **g12**
St. Paul 2,094 **C7**
Schuyler 4,151 **C8**
Scottsbluff 14,156 **C2**
Seward 5,713 **D8**
Sidney 6,010 **C3**
South Sioux City 9,339 **B9**
Stanton 1,603 **C8**
Superior 2,502 **D7**
Syracuse 1,638 **D9**
Tecumseh 1,926 **D9**
Tekamah 1,886 **C9**
Valentine 2,829 **B5**
Valley 1,716 **C9**
Wahoo 3,555 **C9**
Waverly 1,726 **D9**
Wayne 5,240 **B8**
West Point 3,609 **C9**
Wilber 1,624 **D9**
Wymore 1,841 **D9**
York 7,723 **D8**

Statute Miles   5 0 5 10   20   30   40   50   60
Kilometers   5 0 5 15   35   55   75   95

Lambert Conformal Conic Projection
SCALE 1:2,460,000 1 Inch = 39 Statute Miles

Nebraska

POPULATION   1,616,800.
Rank: 36. *Density:* 21 people/mi²
(8.1 people/km²). *Urban:*
62.9%. *Rural:* 37.1%.
INCOME/CAPITA $12,574.
Rank: 23.
ENTERED UNION   March 1, 1867,
37th state.

CAPITAL   Lincoln, 185,800.
LARGEST CITY   Omaha, 367,800.
LAND AREA   76,639 mi²
(198,494 km²).
Rank: 15. *Water area:* 711 mi²
(1,841 km²).
DIMENSIONS   N–S 210 miles,
E–W 415 miles.

ELEVATIONS   *Highest:* In Kimball
County, 5,426 ft
(1,654 m). *Lowest:* In Richardson
County, 840 ft (256 m).
CLIMATE   Hot summers, cold
winters; semiarid in west, more
rain in east.

Nebraska owes its reputation as part of America's great agricultural heartland to the resourcefulness of its settlers, who recognized the prairie as a fertile region. Without their industriousness, Nebraska's abundant potential might have remained undiscovered under miles of tough prairie grass and sagebrush.

The first explorers passing through the Nebraska area looked beyond it to the tempting land and mineral wealth farther west. This section of the so-called Great American Desert appeared to have little to recommend it—no forests, few minerals, and a virtually unbroken expanse of grassland stretching from horizon to horizon. For many decades, Nebraska was merely one section of the transcontinental railroad, linking the East and the West.

But the railroads brought European settlers who recognized the land's possibilities and decided to travel no farther. Soon they had a steel plow strong enough to break through the thick prairie sod, and the settlement of Nebraska was under way. Although semiarid, the state is far from being a desert. In summer, humid tropical air masses from the Gulf of Mexico move far enough north to bring thunderstorms and sudden rain showers. Not long after the first settlers began farming, Nebraska became one of the fastest growing states of its time.

Nebraska's tradition of pioneer resourcefulness continues today. Farmers have quickly adopted mechanized, highly efficient agricultural methods, reducing the number of people needed to till the land. The resulting migration of rural people to the cities has increased Nebraska's urban population and fueled the expanding manufacturing, food-processing, and service industries. Although Nebraska remains a major agricultural state, its people have developed a more diversified economy and will continue to explore new possibilities in the coming decades, meeting the challenges presented by modern economic trends.

In north-central Nebraska, the Sand Hills and the surrounding farmland reflect Nebraskans' successful adaptation to the land. Formed of loose sand, the hills are covered with grass and offer abundant grazing land. The grass holds the soil in place, and because plowing or overgrazing can turn the area into a windblown dust bowl, agriculture is practiced according to conservation guidelines. Nebraskans make the most of the region by using rainfall absorbed by the sand to irrigate areas nearby.

Center-Pivot Irrigation   Beneath Nebraska at a shallow depth lie the water-bearing rock strata called the High Plains Aquifer. Development of the center-pivot irrigation system has enabled farmers far from river-irrigated areas to pump water from the aquifer. Extensive use of the systems in recent decades has dramatically increased Nebraska's cropland.

Circular patterns result in fields irrigated by center-pivot systems.

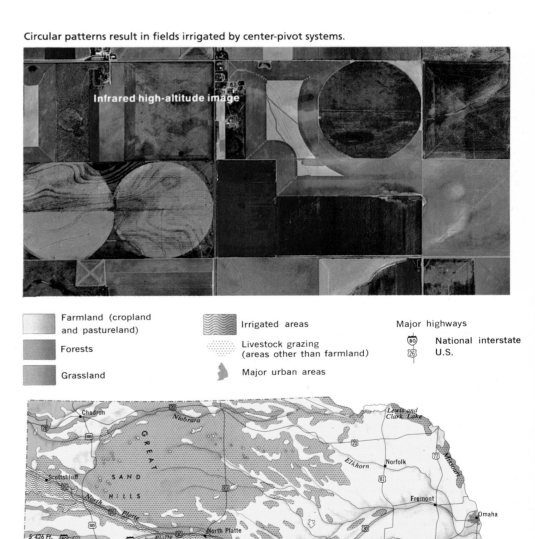

Infrared high-altitude image

One dot represents 5 center-pivot systems

—— Limit of the High Plains Aquifer

Saturated thickness of the aquifer

- 600–1,200 ft
- 200–600 ft
- 0–200 ft

Farmland (cropland and pastureland)

Forests

Grassland

Irrigated areas

Livestock grazing (areas other than farmland)

Major urban areas

Major highways

National interstate

U.S.

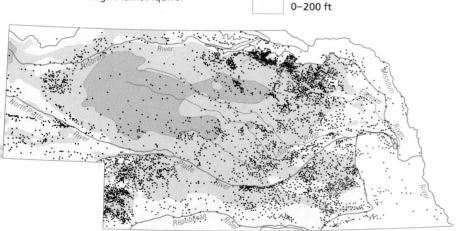

Land Use   Almost all Nebraska's soil has high agricultural potential. In the wetter, eastern part of the state, the land can be employed to maximum capacity more easily. Western Nebraska is semi arid, and intensive farming is practiced mostly on irrigated land. Here, cattle grazing is a productive alternative to grain farming, since it requires much less water.

© RAND MC NALLY & CO.

Cities and Towns

Statute Miles 5 0 5 10 20 30 40 50 60
Kilometers 5 0 5 15 25 35 45 55 65 75

Lambert Conformal Conic Projection
SCALE 1:2,091,000 1 Inch = 33 Statute Miles

A-520535-71
COSMO SERIES NO. DAK.
Copyright by
RAND McNALLY & COMPANY
Made in U.S.A.

Left– LOWER FALLS OF THE YELLOWSTONE, YELLOWSTONE NATIONAL PARK / WYOMING

Below– DOUGLAS FIR, LIVINGSTONE RANGE, GLACIER NATIONAL PARK / MONTANA

Left−PAHOEHOE LAVA, CRATERS OF THE MOON NATIONAL MONUMENT / IDAHO

Above−DEADHORSE POINT STATE PARK, CANYONLANDS / UTAH

TWISTED JUNIPER, BULL PARK OVERLOOK, DINOSAUR NATIONAL MONUMENT / COLORADO

RAINBOW BRIDGE NATIONAL MONUMENT / UTAH

THE WINDOW, MONUMENT VALLEY / ARIZONA

The Southwest

The Southwest

A Land of Infinite Variety

THE SOUTHWEST IS TILTED. IT SLOPES OUT OF the warm Gulf waters with almost incredible gradualness, rising toward the north and west. Dallas, the glitterdome of north Texas, is some three hundred miles inland from the mouth of Galveston Bay, but the land has risen less than 500 feet — less than the height of a modest downtown office building. Follow the Rio Grande two hundred miles upstream to Laredo and you have risen only 440 feet above the sea. Tulsa, in the northeastern corner of the Southwest, is more than five hundred miles from salt water but only 600 feet above the tideline. Westward from the Gulf marshes and the green rivers of eastern Oklahoma, the land rises steadily. The rolling croplands of central Texas and Oklahoma lie 1,000 feet above sea level, the wheat and cattle country of the panhandles is 2,000 feet and higher, rising faster as the New Mexico border is crossed, then soaring into the ridges of the southern Rockies. Between Port Arthur, Texas, and Yuma, Arizona, is a thirteen-hundred-mile territory that progresses from low, flat humid landscape into high, dry vertical country where nothing much is flat except the table-top mesas

and the bottoms of the intermountain valleys.

In the eastern fringe of Oklahoma, the Ouachita Mountains (pronounced Washita) and the Ozark Plateau intrude their pine-covered slopes into the valleys of the Arkansas, Red, and Little rivers. The country here is home to white-tailed deer, raccoons, and big mouth bass. In fact, all of eastern and much of Oklahoma is fishing country.

In Texas, the pine flats of the bayou country lead to open hill croplands, which transmute into the vast central flatness called the Grand Prairie. In Oklahoma the wooded hills are replaced by gently rolling grasslands — the Osage Hills, the Cherokee and Enid plains. From the granite ridges of the Wichitas one looks westward toward those Great Plains. Grass is the dominant natural flora here, commonly a short bluestem giving way to needlegrass where fertility is low. In the Oklahoma Panhandle and north of Amarillo, Texas, this prairie country is called the High Plains. Southward, it's the Staked Plains, the Llano Estacado. Whatever the name, it is a treeless, undulating sea of grass. The Gulf winds rarely bring their moisture here — just enough in the High Plains to grow

Arizona
New Mexico
Oklahoma
Texas

winter wheat.

Farther south in Texas, the Staked Plains are watered by pumps tapping the Ogallala Aquifer, an underground lake that extends into New Mexico and as far north as Nebraska.

In eastern New Mexico the Great Plains are left behind. The horizon no longer fades into the distance. Now it is outlined by the blue shape of mountains. Mountains are the dominant feature of New Mexico. Except for the eastern fringe, no part of the state is without them. Some maps name seventy-three ranges, from Animas to Zuni. They include seven peaks rising above 13,000 feet, eighty-five more than two miles high, and more than three hundred notable enough to warrant names. All are part of the southern Rockies, and they extend all the way south into the empty southwest corner of Texas, giving that state its most spectacular scenery in the Big Bend country.

In New Mexico and Arizona the Chihuahuan Desert flora spreads up the Rio Grande and other valleys for some two hundred miles — almost as far north as Albuquerque — and the Sonoran Desert surrounds the timbered highlands of southern Arizona with its own distinctive species of cacti, grasses, shrubs, and thorn bushes. But deserts are a relatively minor feature of the Southwest's high west side. The story of both states is really the story of mountains, highland plateaus, and sky.

As with Texas and Oklahoma, Arizona and New Mexico generally rise from south to north, but their mountain ridges and plateaus complicate the topography. This high side of the Southwest is rich with such dramatic places, not the least of which is the Grand Canyon, bedazzling its viewers with more than vastness, depth, or layering of colors. Each of its myriad strata seems to erode at a different rate and in a different way; thus its walls are cut and carved into a hundred thousand forms.

No other region of the United States matches the Southwest's wild leap across the spectrum of zones of climate, biology, and geology. Along the eastern margin of Texas, the winds determine the landscape. But as one travels further west, it becomes a matter of altitude. That marked degree of difference is the story of the Southwest.

Overleaf– BLUEBONNETS AND INDIAN PAINTBRUSH, HILL COUNTRY / TEXAS

Left– THUNDERSTORM, PANHANDLE COUNTRY / OKLAHOMA

Center– WICHITA MOUNTAINS NATIONAL WILDLIFE REFUGE / OKLAHOMA

Right– SHEEP'S HEAD, TRUCHAS PEAK, SANGRE DE CRISTO MOUNTAINS / NEW MEXICO

Above– RIO GRANDE RIVER AND SIERRA DEL CARMEN, BIG BEND NATIONAL PARK / TEXAS

Right– SAGUARO CACTUS, PICACHO PEAK STATE PARK / ARIZONA

CANYON DEL MUERTO, CANYON DE CHELLY NATIONAL MONUMENT / ARIZONA

Left– YEI BE CHEI ROCKS, MONUMENT VALLEY NAVAJO TRIBAL PARK / ARIZONA-UTAH

Above– DUNES ABOVE SURF, PADRE ISLAND NATIONAL SEASHORE / TEXAS

Maps of the High Country and Southwest

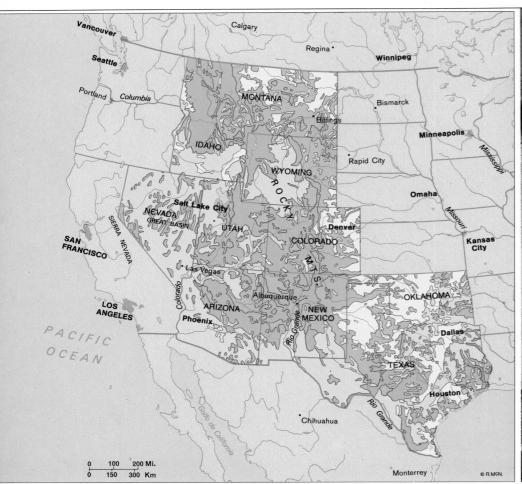

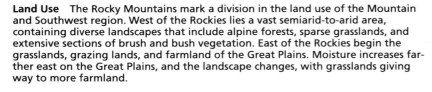

Land Use The Rocky Mountains mark a division in the land use of the Mountain and Southwest region. West of the Rockies lies a vast semiarid-to-arid area, containing diverse landscapes that include alpine forests, sparse grasslands, and extensive sections of brush and bush vegetation. East of the Rockies begin the grasslands, grazing lands, and farmland of the Great Plains. Moisture increases farther east on the Great Plains, and the landscape changes, with grasslands giving way to more farmland.

Preserved in the arid climate of the Southwest are reminders of the native heritage of America. These monuments to ancient Indian cultures display the sophistication, skills, and communal life-style of the country's earliest settlers. Keet Seel, shown here, is a community of cliff dwellings built around one thousand years ago by the Anasazi, the ancestors of modern Pueblo tribes, such as the Hopi and Zuni.

It is not supernatural that so many of America's ghost towns lie within the Mountain and Southwest region. The boomtown, abandoned mine, and battered cattle pen beside a dusty rail spur tell stories that ring true even in modern times. Although these stories might evoke visions of frontier life in the Old West, their significance is less romantic. None of these states can any longer be considered part of a vast frontier. They are crisscrossed with highway, rail, and air routes; and urban areas such as Denver, Dallas, Houston, Phoenix, Salt Lake City, and Las Vegas are true twentieth-century cities in outlook and appearance. The ghost town today is a symbol of the risky boom-to-bust cycle of growth and decline that each of these states faces year after year.

The Mountain and Southwest region is, for the most part, an arid and desolate land of extreme daily and seasonal temperatures; mountain ranges, plains, and wide basins make up the terrain. Within the area lies a great concentration of mineral wealth. An inventory of resources would run from gold and silver, which attracted early fortune seekers; to coal, oil, and gas, which help to fuel the nation; to exotic metals, such as uranium, vanadium, and molybdenum, which are essential to modern manufacturing. However, a state's economic dependence on any one of these resources is risky business. Their markets are distant and volatile, changing with swings in the national economy and the availability of other domestic and foreign supplies. Resource development is frequently intense and brief; towns can grow and die in a short lifetime.

Following the lead of Native Americans, the region's residents have been ingenious in balancing the development of these and other resources to assure survival. Not only do the cities act as bases from which mineral-extraction projects are carried out, but they also form a network for the coordination of development of other resources. The eastern margin of this region is really an outlier of the Midwest's Great Plains, and it shares the plains' agricultural potential for ranching and grain farming. The area's rivers have been dammed and tapped for irrigation water and hydroelectric power. And the warm, dry climate of Arizona, New Mexico, and Nevada is employed to advantage to attract tourists, retirees, high-technology industry, and military installations. Although any of these activities alone may sometimes falter, the Mountain and Southwest states are diversifying economically to counterbalance the economic fluctuation of their individual industries.

Even without the region's material rewards, its beauty would be enough to draw people to it. The sight of the Rockies rising abruptly from Montana's plains at Glacier National Park or the Front Range looming above Colorado's foothills ranks in drama with the Grand Canyon, Monument Valley, and Yellowstone National Park. A growing number of visitors, impressed by the quality of the environment, return to take up permanent residence. Tourism has become a major industry for many of these states.

The Mountain and Southwest region still faces some of the problems that have shaped its development, and the image of the ghost town persists. The states are experiencing rapid growth, and concern for environmental quality is sometimes the first value to wither away. Present knowledge and technological skills can counter the damaging effects of some activities; however, the future development of the region's coal and oil-shale deposits could dwarf almost all previous projects. The potential costs and benefits of such development and the effect on the environment may be among the main concerns of the region in the coming decades. Meanwhile, the states are continuing to work toward economic diversification, countering the uncertainty of their traditional boom-to-bust economies.

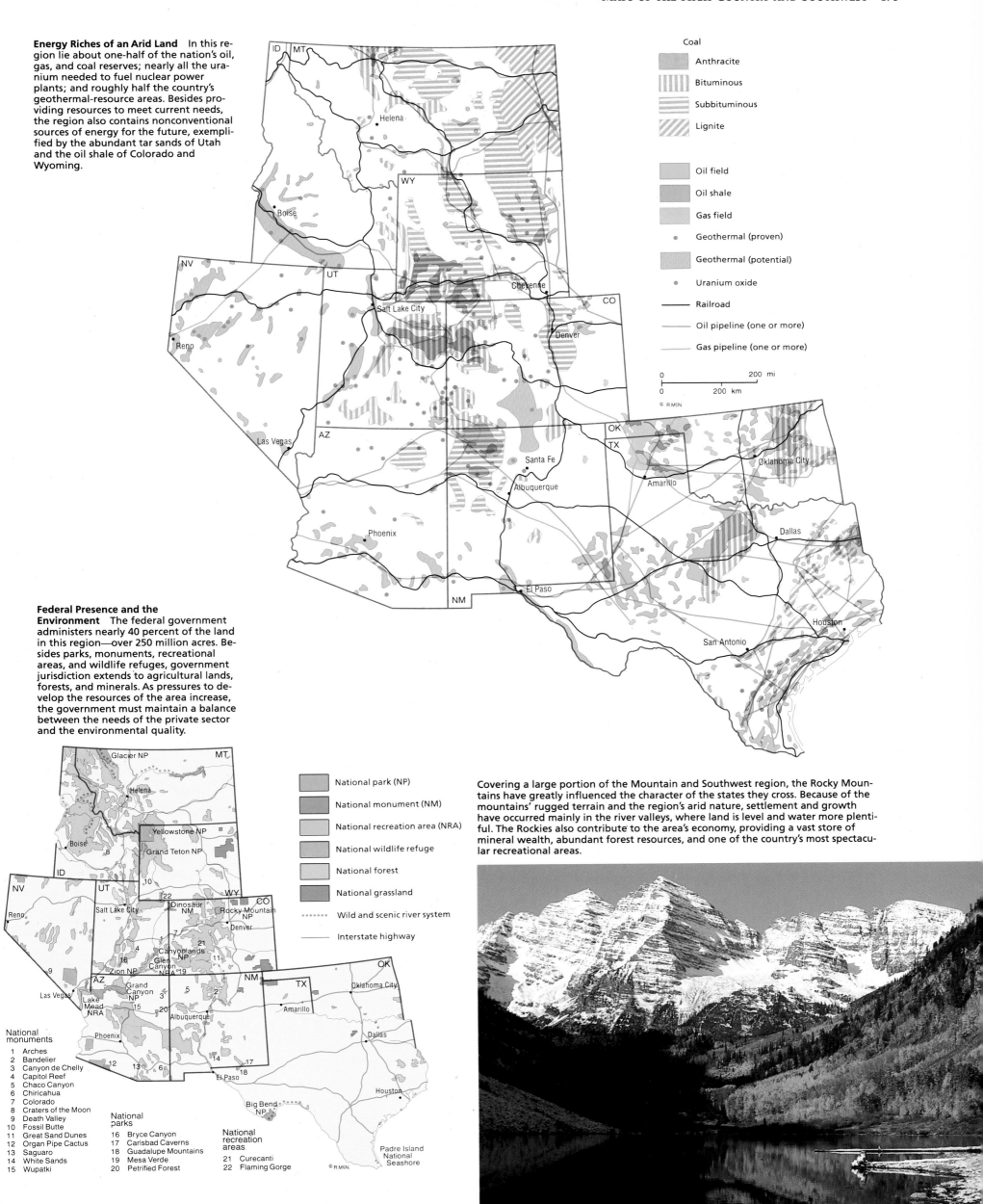

Energy Riches of an Arid Land In this region lie about one-half of the nation's oil, gas, and coal reserves; nearly all the uranium needed to fuel nuclear power plants; and roughly half the country's geothermal-resource areas. Besides providing resources to meet current needs, the region also contains nonconventional sources of energy for the future, exemplified by the abundant tar sands of Utah and the oil shale of Colorado and Wyoming.

Coal
- Anthracite
- Bituminous
- Subbituminous
- Lignite

- Oil field
- Oil shale
- Gas field
- Geothermal (proven)
- Geothermal (potential)
- Uranium oxide
- Railroad
- Oil pipeline (one or more)
- Gas pipeline (one or more)

0   200 mi
0   200 km
© R.McN

Federal Presence and the Environment The federal government administers nearly 40 percent of the land in this region—over 250 million acres. Besides parks, monuments, recreational areas, and wildlife refuges, government jurisdiction extends to agricultural lands, forests, and minerals. As pressures to develop the resources of the area increase, the government must maintain a balance between the needs of the private sector and the environmental quality.

- National park (NP)
- National monument (NM)
- National recreation area (NRA)
- National wildlife refuge
- National forest
- National grassland
- Wild and scenic river system
- Interstate highway

Covering a large portion of the Mountain and Southwest region, the Rocky Mountains have greatly influenced the character of the states they cross. Because of the mountains' rugged terrain and the region's arid nature, settlement and growth have occurred mainly in the river valleys, where land is level and water more plentiful. The Rockies also contribute to the area's economy, providing a vast store of mineral wealth, abundant forest resources, and one of the country's most spectacular recreational areas.

National monuments
1   Arches
2   Bandelier
3   Canyon de Chelly
4   Capitol Reef
5   Chaco Canyon
6   Chiricahua
7   Colorado
8   Craters of the Moon
9   Death Valley
10 Fossil Butte
11 Great Sand Dunes
12 Organ Pipe Cactus
13 Saguaro
14 White Sands
15 Wupatki

National parks
16 Bryce Canyon
17 Carlsbad Caverns
18 Guadalupe Mountains
19 Mesa Verde
20 Petrified Forest

National recreation areas
21 Curecanti
22 Flaming Gorge

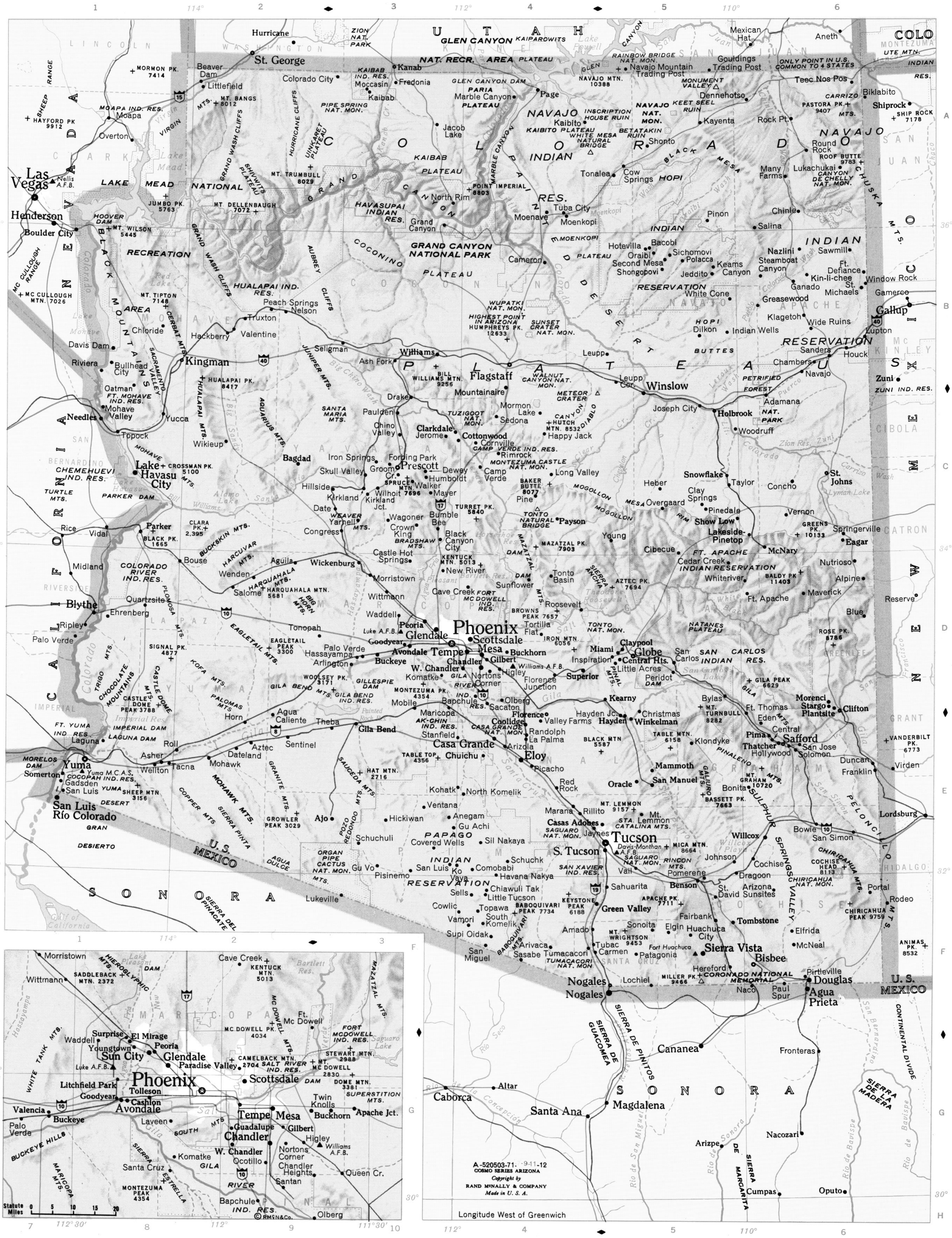

Cities and Towns

Ajo 5,189 **E3**
Apache Junction 9,935 **m9**
Avondale 8,168 **D3**
Bagdad 2,331 **C2**
Benson 4,190 **F5**
Bisbee 7,154 **F6**
Buckeye 3,434 **D3**
Bullhead City 5,000 **B1**
Casa Grande 14,971 **E4**
Casas Adobes 5,300 **E5**
Chandler 29,673 **D4**
Chinle 2,815 **A6**
Chino Valley 2,858 **C3**
Claypool 2,362 **D5**
Clifton 4,245 **D6**
Coolidge 6,851 **E4**
Cottonwood 4,550 **C3**
Douglas 13,058 **F6**
Eagar 2,791 **C6**
Eloy 6,240 **E4**
Flagstaff 34,743 **B4**
Florence 3,391 **D4**
Fort Defiance 3,431 **B6**
Gila Bend 1,585 **E3**
Gilbert 5,717 **D4**
Glendale 97,172 **D3**
Globe 6,886 **D5**
Green Valley 7,999 **F5**
Holbrook 5,785 **C5**
Kayenta 3,343 **A5**
Kearny 2,646 **D5**
Kingman 9,257 **B1**
Lake Havasu City 15,909 **C1**
Mammoth 1,906 **E5**
Mesa 152,453 **D4**
Miami 2,716 **D5**
Nogales 15,683 **F5**
Oracle 2,484 **E5**
Page 4,907 **A4**
Paradise Valley 11,085 **k9**
Parker 2,542 **C1**
Payson 5,068 **C4**
Peoria 12,307 **D3**
Phoenix 789,704 **D3**
Prescott 20,055 **C3**
Riviera 4,500 **B1**
Sacaton 1,951 **D4**
Safford 7,010 **E6**
St. Johns 3,368 **C6**
San Carlos 2,668 **D5**
San Luis 1,946 **E1**
San Manuel 5,443 **E5**
Scottsdale 88,622 **D4**
Sedona 5,368 **C4**
Sells 1,864 **F4**
Show Low 4,298 **C5**
Sierra Vista 24,937 **F5**
Snowflake 3,510 **C5**
Somerton 5,761 **E1**
South Tucson 6,554 **E5**
Sun City 40,505 **k8**
Superior 4,600 **D4**
Taylor 1,915 **C5**
Tempe 106,743 **D4**
Thatcher 3,374 **E6**
Tombstone 1,632 **F5**
Tuba City 5,041 **A4**
Tucson 330,537 **E5**
Wickenburg 3,535 **D3**
Willcox 3,243 **E6**
Williams 2,266 **B3**
Window Rock 2,230 **B6**
Winslow 7,921 **C5**
Yuma 42,481 **E1**

A-520503-71.   9-11-12
COSMO SERIES ARIZONA
Copyright by
RAND McNALLY & COMPANY
Made in U.S.A.

Longitude West of Greenwich

Statute Miles
Kilometers

Lambert Conformal Conic Projection
SCALE 1:2,725,000   1 Inch = 43 Statute Miles

Utah

POPULATION 1,712,400.
Rank: 35.*Density:* 21 people/mi²
(8.1 people/km²).*Urban:*
84.4%.*Rural:* 15.6%.
INCOME/CAPITA $9,739.
Rank: 49.
ENTERED UNION Jan. 4, 1896,
45th state.

CAPITAL Salt Lake City, 165,100.
LARGEST CITY Salt Lake City.
LAND AREA 82,076 mi²
(212,576 km²).
Rank: 12.*Water area:* 2,826 mi²
(7,319 km²).
DIMENSIONS N–S 345 miles,
E–W 275 miles.

ELEVATIONS *Highest:* Kings Peak,
13,528 ft (4,123 m).*Lowest:* In
Washington County, 2,000 ft
(610 m).
CLIMATE Generally very dry. Warm
summers, cold winters. Heaviest
rain in mountains, winter snow.

The dry climate and the unique geologic nature of southeastern Utah largely account for the formation of the region's many fascinating landforms, such as the natural arches shown above. The arches, spires, pinnacles, and alcoves of the area combine to form scenery that is considered to be among the most spectacular in North America.

Demographics A large percentage of Utah's population consists of members of the Church of Jesus Christ of Latter-day Saints, and the importance of children and family in Mormon life is reflected in the state's demographics. Utah is characterized by a higher-than-average birth rate, which in turn contributes to a high population growth rate and a lower-than-average median age. These characteristics affect the state's economy as well as its demographics. Because of a relatively large, young labor force, the state is attractive to businesses, and the growing population creates a market for consumer goods.

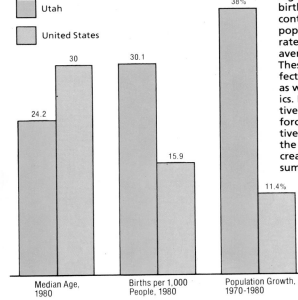

Since pioneer times, Utah has acted as both a pathway and a destination. While thousands crossed the state, headed for adventure and opportunity in the West, many travelers remained to build a home in Utah's beautiful, if somewhat harsh, landscape.

Utah lies along the main route leading from the Great Plains to the Pacific Coast. Modern cross-country travelers using Utah's main highways are actually following paths blazed long ago by pioneers and wagon trains coming from the Mississippi Valley. In the late 1800's, builders of the transcontinental railway laid their tracks along these same early trails. Today, Salt Lake City and its neighbors form the hub of a vast intermontane transportation system stretching from the Rockies to the Sierra Nevada range.

For members of the Church of Jesus Christ of Latter-day Saints—or Mormons—Utah represented a land of religious freedom. The church, founded in New York State in 1830, was persecuted by local religious and legal authorities from Ohio to Illinois and Missouri. Finally driven farther west, the Mormons found biblical parallels between Utah's deserts and salt flats and the land promised to God's Chosen People. They settled in the Great Salt Lake Valley, building a city in the desert. Salt Lake City, in turn, became the center from which Mormons set out to settle other areas in the Southwest. The Mormons are still Utah's largest religious group, and their presence is expressed in the state's social life, including its high marriage and birth rates, and in the spaciously platted towns throughout the region.

Though semiarid, Utah has been blessed with valuable natural resources. It is a leading producer of copper and petroleum, and gold, silver, lead, molybdenum, magnesium, uranium, coal, and salt contribute to the state's economy as well. Utah's natural scenic beauty, its unusual landforms, and its magnificent resort areas draw tourists in increasing numbers, many lured by the challenge of downhill skiing on Utah's steep slopes.

Today, far from being simply a pathway to the West, Utah is a regional center for trade, industry, and commerce. As both a westward route and a destination promising freedom and opportunity, Utah has always played an important role in American life.

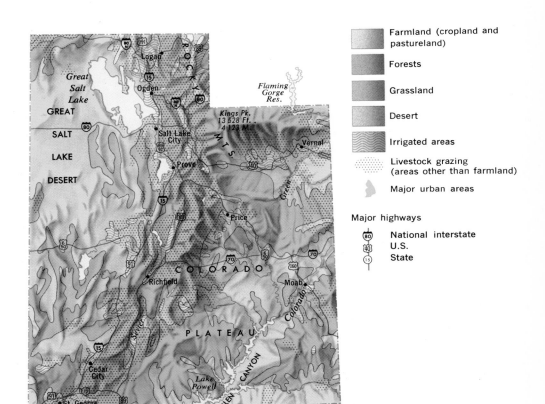

Farmland (cropland and pastureland)

Forests

Grassland

Desert

Irrigated areas

Livestock grazing (areas other than farmland)

Major urban areas

Major highways
- National interstate
- U.S.
- State

Land Use Human settlement and agriculture have followed the baselines of Utah's mountains. Here lie deltas of fertile soils watered by springs from the high mountains. The generally dry climate throughout the state necessitates wise management of moisture provided by precipitation.

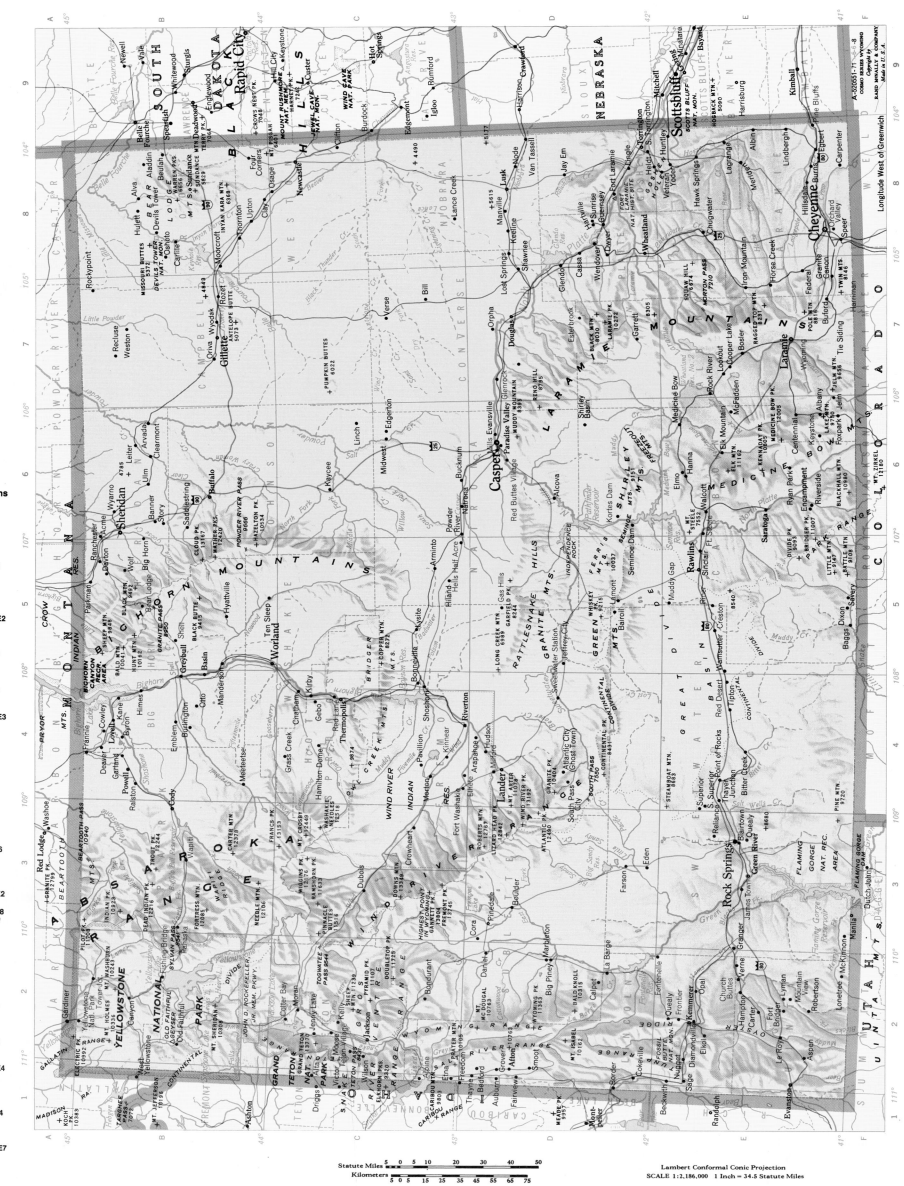

Cities and Towns

Afton 1,481 **D2**
Baggs 433 **E5**
Basin 1,349 **B4**
Big Piney 530 **D2**
Buffalo 3,799 **B6**
Byron 633 **B4**
Casper 51,016 **D6**
Cheyenne 47,283 **E8**
Cody 6,790 **B3**
Cokeville 515 **D2**
Cowley 455 **B4**
Dayton 701 **B5**
Devils Tower 40 **B8**
Diamondville 1,000 **E2**
Douglas 6,030 **D7**
Dubois 1,067 **C3**
Edgerton 510 **C6**
Encampment 611 **E6**
Etna 400 **C1**
Evanston 6,421 **E2**
Evansville 2,335 **D6**
Fort Laramie 356 **D8**
Gillette 12,134 **B7**
Glenrock 2,736 **D7**
Green River 12,807 **E3**
Greybull 2,277 **B4**
Guernsey 1,512 **D8**
Hanna 2,288 **E6**
Hudson 514 **D4**
Jackson 4,511 **C2**
Jeffrey City 400 **D5**
Kemmerer 3,273 **E2**
Lander 7,867 **D4**
Laramie 24,410 **E7**
Lingle 475 **D8**
Lovell 2,447 **B4**
Lusk 1,650 **D8**
Lyman 2,284 **E2**
Marbleton 537 **D2**
Medicine Bow 953 **E6**
Meeteetse 512 **B4**
Midwest 638 **C6**
Mills 2,139 **D6**
Moorcroft 1,014 **B8**
Mountain View 628 **E2**
Newcastle 3,596 **C8**
Orchard Valley 800 **E8**
Paradise Valley 2,300 **D6**
Pine Bluffs 1,077 **E8**
Pinedale 1,066 **D3**
Powell 5,310 **B4**
Ranchester 655 **B5**
Rawlins 11,547 **E5**
Reliance 500 **E3**
Riverton 9,247 **C4**
Rock River 415 **E7**
Rock Springs 19,458 **E3**
Saratoga 2,410 **E6**
Sheridan 15,146 **B6**
Shirley Basin 450 **D6**
Shoshoni 879 **C4**
Sinclair 586 **E5**
South Superior 586 **E4**
Story 700 **B6**
Sundance 1,087 **B8**
Ten Sleep 407 **B5**
Teton Village 200 **C2**
Thermopolis 3,852 **C4**
Torrington 5,441 **D8**
Upton 1,193 **B8**
Wamsutter 681 **E5**
West Laramie 2,000 **E7**
Wheatland 5,816 **D8**
Worland 6,391 **B5**
Yellowstone National Park 350 **B2**

Statute Miles 5 0 5 10 20 30 40 50
Kilometers 5 0 5 15 25 35 45 55 65 75

Lambert Conformal Conic Projection
SCALE 1:2,186,000   1 Inch = 34.5 Statute Miles

Wyoming

POPULATION   500,400.
Rank: 50.*Density:* 5.2 people/mi²
(2.0 people/km²).*Urban:*
62.7%.*Rural:* 37.3%.
INCOME/CAPITA $11,987.
Rank: 29.
ENTERED UNION   July 10, 1890,
44th state.

CAPITAL   Cheyenne, 53,000.
LARGEST CITY   Cheyenne.
LAND AREA   96,988 mi²
(251,198 km²).
Rank: 9.*Water area:* 820 mi²
(2,124 km²).
DIMENSIONS   N–S 275 miles,
E–W 365 miles.

ELEVATIONS   *Highest:* Gannett
Peak, 13,804 ft (4,207 m).*Lowest:*
Along Belle Fourche River, 3,100
ft (945 m).
CLIMATE   Mostly dry with severe
winters and fairly cool summers.
Light summer rain.

Wyoming is one of the last refuges of the fabled American cowboy. Its dude ranches, rodeos, and ranchers on horseback all recreate the atmosphere of the Old West. In preserving this aspect of Wyoming's culture, the state's topography has played a major role. Wide-open spaces and rugged terrain slowed settlement and development, resulting in a sparsely populated state with few of the problems found in heavily urbanized areas.

Because of its harsh terrain, Wyoming was long a thoroughfare rather than a destination. During the gold rush, thousands of prospectors passed through the state on the Oregon Trail, bound for California. The construction of the Union Pacific Railroad across the state led to permanent settlements along the rail route; and in 1868, the Territory of Wyoming was created. Wyoming quickly acquired its reputation for equality by being first to grant women the right to vote, a reputation reinforced in the 1920's when the state elected the first woman governor.

The land shaped not only Wyoming's settlement patterns but its economy as well. The state is a leading mineral producer, with extensive natural resources, including large deposits of oil, coal, natural gas, iron ore, and uranium. In agriculture, sheep and cattle ranching are major industries. And finally, the unsurpassed beauty of Wyoming's natural landscape supports a large-scale tourist business, with people drawn to the Tetons, Jackson Hole, and Yellowstone National Park, among other attractions.

Energy problems in the United States have recently created a new interest in this resource-rich state, and its abundant mineral deposits foretell the great potential of Wyoming's economy. But profits in the energy business fluctuate widely, dependent upon forces outside the state's control, and an energy-based economy is not always a stable one. In addition, many state residents who take pride in the natural beauty of their land are concerned about the effects of development of these resources. For now, however, Wyoming is likely to remain a preserve of mountains, minerals, cattle, and cowboys.

Wyoming's natural environment supports a large variety of animal life, both domesticated and wild. In addition to cattle, grazing horses are a common sight, such as those shown here in Grand Teton National Park. Wild areas provide refuge for large animals such as elk, grizzly and black bears, antelopes, mountain lions, and lynxes plus a wide range of small animals and birds, including bald and golden eagles.

Thrust Zone Minerals

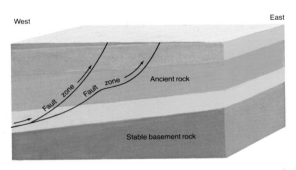

Wyoming's heritage of mineral riches is the result of millions of years of geologic activity. About 550 to 325 million years ago, massive and gradual earth movements caused rock layers containing the basic elements for oil and gas to move over stable basement rock.

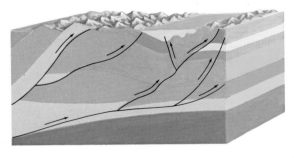

Around 325 to 225 million years ago, pressures inside the earth pushed these rocks together, causing faulting and folding, with rocks thrust over one another to form mountain ranges. As these mountains eroded, more sediments were deposited, containing elements with potential for oil and gas formation.

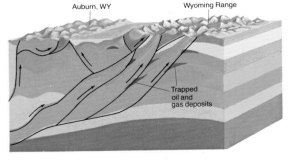

From about 225 million years ago to the present, continued pressure has been converting these basic elements into oil and gas deposits. Today, the nation looks to southwest Wyoming's Thrust Zone to ensure energy supplies for the coming years.

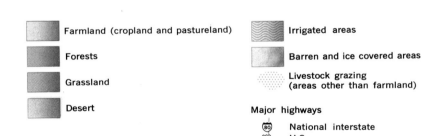

Farmland (cropland and pastureland)	Irrigated areas
Forests	Barren and ice covered areas
Grassland	Livestock grazing (areas other than farmland)
Desert	

Major highways

National interstate
U.S.

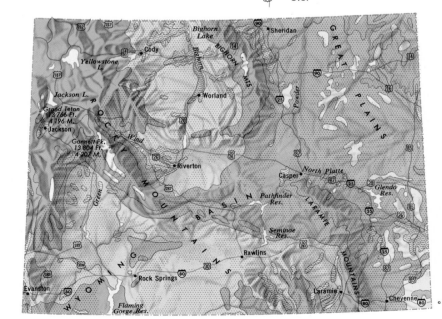

Land Use   Much of Wyoming's land is used for agriculture, mainly sheep and cattle ranching. Modern conservation practices are widely employed, including regulation of irrigation with computers.

BIG SUR COASTLINE / CALIFORNIA

DUMONT DUNES, MOJAVE DESERT / CALIFORNIA

Above– RAIN FOREST, ECOLA STATE PARK / OREGON

Left– SHROUDED GIANTS, SEQUOIA NATIONAL PARK / CALIFORNIA

Right– PROXY FALLS, CASCADE RANGE / OREGON

Far Right– SURGE AND FLOW, CARMEL COAST / CALIFORNIA

Below– MOUNT RAINIER FROM THE NORTHEAST / WASHINGTON

Above– CASCADE AT LOW WATER, ROGUE RIVER GORGE / OREGON

Right– ON CAPE FLATTERY / WASHINGTON

ALASKA RANGE REFLECTED IN WONDER LAKE, DENALI NATIONAL PARK / ALASKA

Washington

POPULATION 4,548,900. *Rank:* 19.*Density:* 68 people/mi² (26 people/km²).*Urban:* 73.5%.*Rural:* 26.5%. **INCOME/CAPITA** $13,650. *Rank:* 10. **ENTERED UNION** Nov. 11, 1889, 42nd state.	**CAPITAL** Olympia, 31,200. **LARGEST CITY** Seattle, 487,900. **LAND AREA** 66,512 mi² (172,265 km²). *Rank:* 20.*Water area:* 1,627 mi² (4,214 km²). **DIMENSIONS** N–S 230 miles, E–W 340 miles.	**ELEVATIONS** *Highest:* Mount Rainier, 14,410 ft (4,392 m).*Lowest:* Pacific Ocean shoreline, sea level. **CLIMATE** Cool summers, mild winters along coast; hot summers, cold winters, dry on inland plateau.

Washington is a study in the interplay of geography and economy. Both its commerce and industry have been shaped by the state's far-northwest location and its endowment of natural resources.

Washington's location makes it a trade and transportation center whose influence extends far beyond its shores. In many ways, the state serves as Alaska's principal port of call, a harbor for northwest Canada, and an outpost for Japan and other Asian countries doing business with the United States.

Yet Washington's key resource is water—not only Puget Sound and the Pacific Ocean, but its many inland rivers. Both the Snake and the Columbia rivers are important sources of hydroelectric power and irrigation water, and because the Cascade Range divides Washington into wet and semiarid regions, geography determines how this water will be used. Hydroelectric power drives the major centers of industry along the western coastal areas while irrigation water is channeled to the croplands of the Columbia Plateau in the eastern regions. The state's water resources create an economy of unusual breadth and variety. Its production of aircraft and aerospace hardware in the west is as well known as its fruit and potato crops in the east. Inland wheat harvests are as important to national markets as the state's coastal shipbuilding.

Despite Washington's economic mastery of its geographical divisions, the state faces problems nearly as volatile as its Mount St. Helens. Markets for many of Washington's more important products—such as aircraft, ships, lumber and pulp, fruit, and grain—fluctuate widely from year to year, leaving the state vulnerable to forces outside its borders. Further, the federal government holds title to a major share of Washington's land and has invested heavily in irrigation, hydroelectric projects, the Hanford atomic energy facility, and the aerospace and shipbuilding industries. Changes in these commitments could affect Washington's control over its resources and its economy.

Yet even with these problems, Washington remains an important shipping center not only for the Pacific Coast but for countries halfway around the world. The state's rich industrial and natural resources will help it meet the many challenges of the future.

Mount Shuksan is typical of many mountains of the northern Cascades. The area's topography is often compared to that of the Alps, and the mountains are a major tourist attraction. But the high, rugged peaks affect more than Washington's beauty; they also act as an economic and climatic barrier, making transportation difficult and keeping moist Pacific winds from reaching the state's interior. On the positive side, the waterfalls and rivers provide water supplies and hydropower, and the tree-covered slopes are a source of timber.

Volcanic Forces   The volcanic eruption of Mount St. Helens is a reminder of the forces affecting the lands circling the Pacific Ocean. Moving sections of the earth's crust called plates meet in these areas. At the zone of contact, the Pacific Plate is pushed into hotter depths and partly converted to melted rock, or magma. As magma rises, it erupts, and in time a series of volcanic mountains is formed.

Land Use   Although the farms of eastern Washington are blocked from much eastward-moving precipitation by the Cascades, the entire state is still influenced by the Pacific Ocean, which has a moderating effect on the climate.

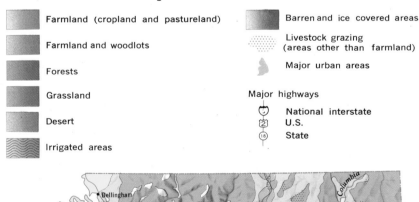

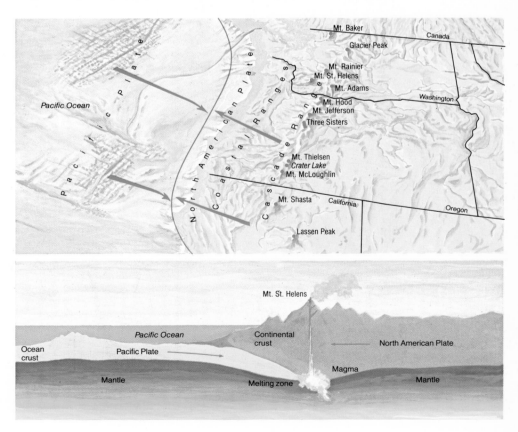

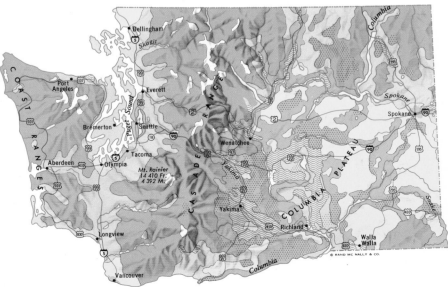

United States
Mileage & Driving-Time Map

Mileages and Driving Times Copyright ©1987
by Rand McNally-TDM, Inc.

EXPLANATION

277 Light numerals indicate mileage in statute miles.

7:55 Bold numerals indicate driving time.

Driving time shown is approximate under normal conditions. Consideration has been given to topography, number of towns along route, congested urban areas, and the federally imposed maximum 55 m.p.h. speed law.

Allowances should be made for night driving and unusually fast or slow drivers.